"From the International Rescue Committee to Lincoln Center, Reynold Levy has successfully led some of the world's most influential nonprofit institutions and also worked as an advisor and board member to major corporations. Drawing on his extraordinary experiences, Levy has written a must-read guide for anyone seeking to build a meaningful career."

—**Steven Swartz**, president and CEO,
Hearst Communications

"As Reynold Levy knows from his multifaceted experience in leading first-class institutions, human talent is the single best indicator of excellence. In *Start Now*, he brilliantly offers his perspective on how to prepare for a rewarding career. Whether you are a newcomer to the workplace, or seeking a different position, this source of value-added advice is a must-read."

—**Tracy R. Wolstencroft**, former president and CEO,
National Geographic Society, and president,
CEO, and chairman, Heidrick & Struggles

# START NOW

January 2020

For Bill

Who took a lead in birthing a
banking enterprise from
scratch in our country's
largest city.
It pulsates. It thrives.
And, we are just getting started.

May thanks and best wishes

Reynold Levy

# START NOW

## Because That Meaningful Job Is Out There, Just Waiting For You

## REYNOLD LEVY

RosettaBooks®

NEW YORK 2020

First edition published 2020 by RosettaBooks

Cover design by Mimi Bark
Interior design by Jay McNair

ISBN-13 (print): 978-1-9481-2254-2
ISBN-13 (ebook): 978-0-7953-5278-2

Library of Congress Cataloging-in-Publication Data

Names: Levy, Reynold, author.
Title: Start now : because that meaningful job
is out there, just waiting for you / Reynold Levy.
Description: First edition. | New York : RosettaBooks, 2020. |
Includes bibliographical references and index.
Identifiers: LCCN 2019035945 (print) | LCCN 2019035946 (ebook) |
ISBN 9781948122542 (hardcover) | ISBN 9780795352782 (ebook)
Subjects: LCSH: Vocational guidance. | Career development. |
Job hunting. | Job satisfaction.
Classification: LCC HF5381 .L3567 2020 (print) |
LCC HF5381 (ebook) | DDC 650.14—dc23
LC record available at https://lccn.loc.gov/2019035945

RosettaBooks®

www.RosettaBooks.com
Printed in the United States of America

*For Elizabeth and Justin*
*with love and gratitude*

# Contents

# Acknowledgments

*Start Now* originated with two questions.

If hundreds of friends, acquaintances, business associates, clients, and students seem to benefit from my advice about shaping their professional future, then why not capture the lessons learned in writing?

If dozens of employers ask me to help guide them in their quest to recruit, retain, and motivate key personnel, then why not revert to the printed page, distilling the advice I readily offered?

Between the many thin-lined white and yellow legal pads filled with ideas, references, research, and case examples, to the book now in your hands, friends appeared, offering their help.

Some of those volunteer assistants are themselves accomplished writers and editors. Each reviewed the manuscript in various stages of development. Each provided perspectives and critiques, willingly and generously. I am very grateful to them, one and all.

Kara Medoff Barnett, Ed Bligh, Shilla Kim-Parker, Dick Martin, Nessa Rapoport, Henry Wainhouse, and Sabrina Yudelson are not just able readers and critics possessed of high standards. They provided what every author also needs: encouragement and cheerleading.

Ken Auletta, Lee Bollinger, Jennifer Homans, Tim McClimon, Indra Nooyi, David Rubenstein, Steven Swartz, and Tracy Wolstencroft were also discerning reviewers of the manuscript. They cheerfully interrupted the rhythm of very busy lives to spend dedicated time with my work. I am the beneficiary of their caring and insightful views.

My lifelong best friend, Bart Friedman, offered a thorough and thoughtful assessment. The care of his commentary is illustrative of how generous he has been to me over the course of the six decades we have known one another.

It is no wonder, then, that *Start Now* is a better book for their thoughtful suggestions and motivational messages. It is no wonder, then, that I decided to answer those two questions affirmatively.

My wife, Elizabeth, and my son, Justin, did not hesitate to tell me how this book might improve. If you like what you are about to read, credit their benevolent intervention. If you harbor reservations, rest assured, they and their critical companions whom I have named are to be held blameless.

My literary agent, Jim Levine, knows his way around books and authors. He is a peerless coach. I am delighted that we could reunite to collaborate on this project.

Arthur Klebanoff is a rare creature in publishing and a new figure in my life. In a sometimes insular, thin-skinned, self-satisfied profession, he is an exception. Arthur actually advocates for his authors. He believes the books they generate should reflect their points of view and not his own. No writer could ask for a more reliable, supportive ally. I am fortunate to have found my way to him.

Arthur's colleague, Brian Skulnik, was an adept, adroit, and versatile managing editor. He rendered what is often a very tedious process into an enjoyable, collaborative experience. Working together with his colleague, Michelle Weyenberg, I was reminded of all that it takes to transform 55,000 words of copy into something magical, otherwise known as a handsome book.

Kelsey Orens, a talented executive at The Walt Disney Company who is based in Los Angeles, typed this book in manuscript form with skill, finesse, and attention to detail. She accommodated her schedule to mine, often working diligently under deadline pressure. She conducted research and is involved in the marketing and sales plan for *Start Now*. I am exceedingly grateful to her for the constancy and purposefulness of our bicoastal relationship.

# Start Now

### Because the Worst Time to Look for a Meaningful Job Is When You Need One

---

## Introduction

Write what you know about. Write when something makes a strong claim on you.

That's the universal advice offered to authors.

Be useful.

That's the siren call of service to others. It ricochets in the minds of millions of Americans of all ages, myself included.

*Start Now* is the result of these convictions.

It is addressed to all who wish to enjoy not only a productive livelihood, but a life that assists those in need. From family and friends to the vulnerable and the ill. From your fellow employees in the workplace to neighbors and members of your broader community. From public and nonprofit institutions that cry out for strengthening to noble causes of all kinds in search of committed activists.

A fair question about a book of advice is, "Why pay attention to the author?"

More than fifty years after my first job, and still very active, I have been fortunate to be engaged at the highest levels of many nonprofit and private enterprises. The board members and supporters of the nonprofits I have professionally led or helped govern as a trustee are themselves important figures in commercial firms, of every variety, in charitable organizations, foundations, and government. I have advised and mentored hundreds of people on their career paths as they have confronted diverse challenges and opportunities. I have been part of the search, as an employer and as a consultant, for hundreds of job candidates at all stages of their working lives and on every rung of the professional ladder.

To all of these interactions, I have brought my own life experience. It has been filled with meaningful work and fulfilling voluntary activities.

I have helped a broad coalition of service and advocacy groups protect the poor from draconian state and city budget cuts when I served as the executive director of the task force on the New York City fiscal crisis. I have been the chief executive of the nation's oldest, largest, and most comprehensive community center, the 92nd Street Y. I was the architect and first president of the AT&T Foundation, then the nation's most formidable corporate philanthropic enterprise. Later, I assumed more expansive roles in public and government relations for this Fortune 10 firm, both in the United States and around the world.

From there, I was appointed president of the International Rescue Committee, an essential and influential provider of resettlement and relief services to refugees located in more than thirty poor and war-torn countries.

I then became president of Lincoln Center for the Performing Arts, America's first and the largest and most prominent enterprise of its kind, anywhere. Its award-winning physical transformation and the raising of over $1.5 billion to finance it, together with Lincoln Center's singular cultural programs, were highlights of my tenure.

After thirteen years in that capacity, most recently I was invited to become the president of the Robin Hood Foundation.

While holding these posts, I also was retained as a consultant, author, professor, and public speaker and as the lead outside director of First Republic Bank. In addition, I have been actively involved in charitable and philanthropic enterprises of all kinds, as a trustee of many nonprofits and foundations, as a volunteer, and as a donor.

These diverse incarnations have left me in a position to help many people find meaningful work and to assist them in leading productive and fulfilling lives. What I learned, the experiences I enjoyed, the relationships I established, and the situations I encountered all have informed the counseling it has been my privilege to provide.

> Help me if you can, I'm feeling down.
> And I do appreciate your being round.
> Help me get my feet back on the ground.
> Won't you please, please help me?[1]

For the better part of my adulthood, I have answered the call for help so memorably expressed by the Beatles. I have willingly responded to everything from plaintive requests to insistent pleas for guidance. "I feel stuck. What should I do now? Can you help me identify and then compete for highly desirable jobs?" Those are the questions most often put to me in a variety of forms.

By high school and college students already anticipating their first full-time job. By newcomers to the workplace. By white-collar employees in transition to entirely new fields of endeavor. By prosperous midcareer adults who wish to move from professional success to social consequence. By those afflicted with burnout, boredom, stress, even midlife crisis. By careers shortened due to the physical punishment they inflict: professional dancers, athletes of all stripes, and construction workers are conspicuous among the victims. By the casualties of totally unexpected layoffs.

These are just some of the circumstances that usher friends, acquaintances, colleagues, former students, trustees, and donors to my open door.

Because I have fostered professional development across multiple sectors—arts and culture, business and government, for-profit and not-for-profit—many of those helped think of me as their career coach. In *Start Now*, I will convey the best advice I've offered to help people land not just any job, but a post that fits like a bespoke suit. Your talents, values, occupational trajectory, and, most important, desire to lead a life that matters deserve no less.

After all, in 2017, 21 percent of all American workers—more than one in five—changed jobs, while companies spent over $200 billion to find employees to fill open positions and tens of billions of dollars more to train them.[2] Odds are that in the next five years, you, your parents, children, close friends, and colleagues will all be looking for new employment.

This desire to move up quickly or to leave a current position for a better one is said to be especially strong among millennials. Burdened by unprecedented student debt, subject to peer and parental pressures to succeed, and surrounded by a start-up culture, university graduates are understandably not fond of deferred gratification. The business environment that surrounds them rivets attention on quarterly results. The information environment places a premium on frequent, often instantaneous communication of news and opinion. Social media, including Facebook and LinkedIn, prominently displays what peers are accomplishing as they move to more demanding, prestigious, and well-compensated assignments.

The calls to me requesting help are not at all surprising, given how much turbulence there is in the employment marketplace. Shifts to new jobs, by choice or necessity, remain a fact of life for millions of Americans every year.

I know of only a few ways you can favorably influence others and help guide their professional and personal lives. You can teach, formally in school settings and on the job as boss, mentor, or colleague. You can be part of a team whose members learn from one another on their way to realizing a common objective, or to falling short of doing so. You can offer consulting services, responding to the expressed needs of clients. And you can commit to writing what you have learned over a lifetime of experience, hopefully for the benefit of others. I have been blessed to serve in all of these roles.

*Start Now* is my final way of offering a contribution to those looking for more meaningful, soul-satisfying, or lucrative work.

While it can guide you to securing an entry-level position in government, a commercial firm, or a nonprofit, *Start Now* doesn't stop there.

It offers recommendations on advancing a career with your current employer, while keeping alert to external market opportunities.

Look to *Start Now* for advice on how best to move up from junior accountant to chief financial officer, from special events manager to a position in city hall, from fact checker and freelance writer to assistant editor, from public relations staffer to managing director for external affairs, and from a member in good standing of a sales team to senior vice president for sales and marketing.

Such journeys inside one employer or in traveling from one to another can be expedited, elongated, or stymied. Much depends on how you combine ambition with diplomacy and skill acquisition with a results orientation. Successfully moving up or moving out to ascend elsewhere requires a judicious blend of applied intelligence and the capacity to attract colleagues who enjoy working at your side.

My own shifts within and between organizations and the changes in subject matter that they addressed are not unique to me. They are the product of discipline and workplace habits that you can adopt or modify to suit your own needs. They are also the result of caring mentors and supervisors, gifted women and men from whom I have learned much and who believed in me. And there is always the element of serendipity, discovering a promising possibility by recognizing that you are in the right place at the right time.

Drawing on my career and advice to others, I will help you to think about your future creatively and to prepare for it resourcefully. How to network naturally and adeptly. How to interview effectively. I will offer you a recipe for moving up in an appealing organization or moving out gracefully to a better position elsewhere. Such transitions can be part of a natural process. They needn't become tension-filled episodes in life. Many a crisis at work is avoidable.

The professional voyage you undertake can be enlightening and fun rather than nerve-racking. As much as possible, you need to take control, to be in command of your own career development.

The guidance I present is relevant no matter what the stage of your professional journey. It will offer you actionable ideas for purposefully occupying the last quarter of your life. Even if you are truly at career's end, when beaches, books, and golf courses beckon, what follows will help your children and grandchildren prepare themselves for a life of personal and vocational commitment.

The driving force of this book and of a successful life is captured in the title—*Start Now*. Why? Because the best time to find a meaningful job is when you don't need one. Otherwise, you run the risk of being unable to quickly recover from being dismissed, demoted, or marginalized at your current post. With nothing concrete in mind for the future, confusion and disarray can dominate your life. Your self-confidence can shatter. The sense of security and stability you possessed is suddenly gone. Your social standing is threatened. And the pathways to new and rewarding work are beclouded. I know. All of this has happened to me.

How to avoid such circumstances and what to do if they should ever arise are among the subjects of *Start Now*. Another is determining whether an employer is one with which you wish to be associated. Learning about the culture of the organization, how it treats personnel and what it values most in promoting veterans and hiring newcomers will help you to decide where and whether to pursue a vacancy.

For the moment, let's begin with the upbeat observation that in searching for an exciting new job, you, the unemployed, may be pushing through an open door. After all, businesses and nonprofits are struggling to recruit and retain talent, often at great cost and with disappointing results. Supply and demand can match up agreeably in the employment marketplace. Your objective is to become a case example of victory as employers exercise their options in the ebb and flow of the hiring process.

Your successful quest will satisfy not just personal needs, but those of your future employer.

*Start Now* is an invitation to join me and many others in preparing for your own lifelong travel experience. For these trips, you can pack lightly. There will be no need to check a bag at the airport. No passport or visa is required. But do bring with you a spirit of adventure, a curiosity about how organizations achieve results, an eagerness to learn, a willingness to enter unfamiliar territory and to form entirely new relationships.

Oh, and do carry aboard two other qualities: resilience and a sense of humor. For along the way there will be setbacks, detours, and disappointments. How you manage them is as important as handling good news gracefully. Also absolutely necessary are hard work and persistence. Those who exhibit these attributes enjoy a distinct advantage in any competition for that coveted job.

## What to Do, Whom to Be

*What do you want to do when you grow up?*

Is there a more frequent question asked of children and adolescents?

For some parents, important questions literally begin with the birth of their children. Shall it be private or public school for my newborn? If the former, what are your preferences and how do you begin to prepare in the competition for admission? If the latter, where do you need to live to qualify your child for entry, and should you consider mainstream or charter schools or both? Trust me, one hasn't lived until one has composed a glowing recommendation for a three-year-old's admission to preschool at Horace Mann or the 92nd Street Y. At least in Manhattan, that's how early families are introduced to the rigorous competition of finding the right school for their child.

Of course, there are decisions to reach about (community) college. To which shall you apply? How much should your choices be governed by informed guesses about the kinds of jobs that might be available to you after graduation? What determines the major course of study you will pursue? Realistically, how important is a (community) college to your career prospects? And, in any event, how are those college years best spent to prepare you not only for meaningful work, but for a worthy, fulfilling life?

As student debt exceeds all credit card liabilities in America, approaching no less than $1.7 trillion, is it any wonder that adults, parents most particularly, wish to know how their kids and significant others plan to earn a living?

Still, this standard line of inquiry—what do you want to do when you grow up—is often misplaced and premature.

First, it is a tough question for most to answer definitively without sufficient knowledge, experience, and exposure to job opportunities.

Second, the question assumes there is a single response to a life-long challenge.

Most American adults will hold at least seven full-time positions before retirement. Whatever answer each provides now must be provisional and tentative, subject to actual time on the job, to real-life encounters at various workplaces.

Third, a more important and enduring issue than what you want to do is whom you wish to become. The former is about how you'll earn a paycheck. The latter concerns your character and values. What kind of husband or wife, mother or father, aunt or uncle do you aspire to be? How will you contribute to the community in which you live, or help to solve the problems of the less fortunate in your midst? What is your role and obligation as an American citizen?

Our overriding concern for securing a paying job, for worldly success, runs the risk of neglecting who we will come to be in other vital parts of life as family members, as neighbors, as patriots.

After all, what you do to satisfy monthly bills is only a part of your identity, a piece of what brings genuine satisfaction in life.

David Brooks, the *New York Times* columnist and best-selling author, usefully refers to the difference between "résumé values" and "eulogy values." Taking the long view, how will you wish to reflect on the way in which you conducted your life and its impact on others? How will friends, colleagues, associates, and family members think about your brief time on earth? What will be your legacy? Brooks observes that the way in which those closest to you feel is almost always far more consequential than the business success you might have enjoyed. How you have treated others and your favorable influence on them causes pecuniary success to fade in significance.[3]

The key question those well-intentioned friends and relatives should be asking is not what you want to do, but whom you wish to be as you mature.

*Start Now* distills the key lessons I have learned about these considerations from decades of pro bono consulting and influence wielding. These lessons are shaped in a form intended to be helpful to students, parents, and adults looking beyond what it takes to make ends meet. More than likely, you are also searching for energizing and fulfilling challenges, at work and in life.

The narrative flows from this ironclad truth: the absolute worst time to look for a first or next job is when you need one. Just-in-time desirable vacancies are extremely rare. Advance preparation is critically important.

## The Attractive Nonprofit Sector

Thinking about your future broadly is a good start. Do not prematurely or inadvertently rule out entire fields of endeavor or major areas of productive and rewarding activity.

In sheer numbers, most employment can be found in the realms first of business and then of government. But the nonprofit sector has also become an important marketplace for those with talent looking to enjoy a purpose-driven working life. It is large, sprawling, and filled with opportunity for a start-up job or for a fully satisfying, lifelong career. Its pay scales and working conditions are continuously improving. Employment in what are legally referred to as 501(c)(3) organizations no longer requires taking a vow of poverty. And the skills and capabilities that nonprofits both seek and nurture are largely transferable for those who wish to gravitate to commercial or governmental assignments.

Why is this formidable sphere of American life so shrouded in mystery? Its component parts are many, varied, and arrayed across a wide range of fields. What they have in common is not well understood. Few of its constituent institutions, numbering in the hundreds of thousands, recruit for new hires at colleges and universities or job fairs. Few advertise their vacancies in general-purpose publications. Far less is widely known about them. While there are specialized and expensive-to-purchase trade publications addressed to subjects like philanthropy or higher education, there is no *Forbes*, *Fortune*, *Bloomberg Businessweek*, *Barron's*, *Crain's*, or the *Wall Street Journal* that covers nonprofits as comprehensively, assiduously, and critically as is the case for business. Few, if any, full-time reporters anywhere are assigned to a nonprofit beat, a standard practice for the coverage of private and public companies and government agencies.

And yet this general nonprofit domain is chock-full of employment opportunities of all kinds. Do not fail to consider them alongside their better known for-profit and public-sector counterparts.

For the last three decades, the voluntary, mission-oriented so-called Third Sector has grown faster than either the commercial economy or the government. It now comprises about 7 percent of the gross domestic product and owns about 10 percent of the value of all of the nation's real estate. It employs some seventeen million Americans, representing one out of every seven white-collar jobs. It spent roughly $1.4 trillion in 2018, some $428 billion of which came in the form of tax-deductible gifts to tax-exempt institutions.[4]

Because it is service focused and labor intensive, few of its jobs are exportable. Because it is heavily concentrated in health, education, social services, the arts, the environment, advocacy, and faith-based organizations, this realm of the economy is not only inoculated against outsourcing to other nations, it has also proven to be largely recession-proof.

Nonprofits mobilize energy and resources. It is estimated that more Americans give funds and/or volunteer time to charity than vote, even in a presidential election. Indeed, some four million Americans serve on a nonprofit board of directors. Often, these institutions draw the interest and energy of leading citizens who donate their time, talent, and treasure willingly and with a great deal of pleasure and satisfaction.

We generally consider commercial enterprises to be strong and solid, whereas nonprofits are regarded as fragile and unstable. But of the Fortune 500 firms existing in 1955, only 12 percent remained viable entities by 2015. The other 88 percent had gone bankrupt, been acquired by other entities, or been replaced by more thriving firms. Do you remember Armstrong Rubber? Cone Mills? Hines Lumber? American Motors? Eastman Kodak? Brown Shoe? Studebaker? Collins Radio? Detroit Steel? Zenith Electronics? National Sugar Refining? Enron? WorldCom? They have gone the way of the corporate dinosaur.

The fact that nearly 90 percent of Fortune 500 companies have disappeared, merged, or contracted over the last sixty-five years demonstrates a healthy market disruption, sometimes referred to as "creative destruction," a term invented by the economist Joseph Schumpeter. Those long-forgotten names have been replaced by the likes of Facebook, eBay, Home Depot, Microsoft, WeWork, Google, Apple, Netflix, Amazon, and Uber.

For the dynamic American economy, this is all healthy and normal. For the newly unemployed American caught up in and victimized by this free-enterprise activity, not so much.

By comparison, nonprofits seem enduring. In higher education, for example, some are older than the nation itself. Think Harvard (1640) and Columbia (1754) Universities, among other institutions of higher education. And many have celebrated longevity far greater than their for-profit counterparts ever come close to reaching. In my hometown of New York City, New York University

(1831), Columbia Presbyterian (1868), Collegiate (1638), and the 92nd Street Y (1874) are all well over a century old, as are the Metropolitan Opera (1880) and the New York Philharmonic (1842). Catholic Charities is seventy-five years old, and the Federation of Jewish Philanthropies just celebrated its hundredth anniversary in 2017. Many more octogenarian and older charities could be named. The list is impressively long.

Nonprofits are not only durable; they continue to grow at a rapid pace. According to the US Department of Labor's Bureau of Labor Statistics, from the prerecession year of 2007 to 2016, nonprofit employment increased by nearly 17 percent, while for-profit employment climbed by less than 5 percent. This phenomenon of the Third Sector outpacing the commercial realm in terms of employment took place all across America.[5]

These trends solidify nonprofit organizations as the third-largest workforce in America, behind just retail trade and manufacturing. Not only does the nonprofit sector account for the nation's third-largest payroll, its total wages exceed that of most other US industries, including construction, transportation, and finance.

What's more, nonprofits constitute over 90 percent of employment in American private higher educational institutions, 84 percent of employment in private hospitals, 85 percent of employment in private elementary and secondary schools, and 42 percent in private social assistance organizations.

Beyond the size, scope, duration, and employment potency of these Third Sector institutions, consider purpose. Prevent and cure disease. Reduce poverty. Expand education. Relieve misery. Build housing. Strengthen social services. Protect immigrants and refugees. Promote arts and culture. Combat climate change. Generate original research. Spur innovation.

Can you think of a major social cause of consequence—race relations, women's rights, civil rights, gay rights, marriage equality, environmental preservation, consumer protection, food insecurity among them—for which Third Sector institutions were not in the lead?

It is no surprise, then, that some of the nation's most gifted doctors, executives, intellectuals, engineers, lawyers, and social activists find their way to employment in this consequential part of the American economy.

And while *Start Now* is hardly confined to nonprofits, it offers a map and a compass to help today's job applicants find their way to employment that elevates, dignifies, and ennobles.

If this book were not entitled *Start Now*, it could just as well have been called *Never Stop* or *Persistence Wins*. Actually, my preferred second choice in title is *Hustle: The End of Either/Or*.

## The End of Either/Or

The spirit that infuses the search for meaningful work is one of energy, determination, purposefulness, and resilience.

You can be devoted to your current assignment at work *and* explore broadening and elevating it.

You can fully discharge your obligations to your current employer *and* take on part-time assignments *and* significant forms of public service.

You can begin your career in any of the three sectors *and*, with the proper preparation, move to another.

Over time, it is perfectly possible to strike a balance between the demands of the workplace *and* commitments to home life.

Call a halt to either/or thinking.

Keep *both* in the forefront of your mind.

Doing so will entail very busy days, crowded calendars, and a diversified portfolio of obligations. It will mean communicating in many ways with a host of friends, acquaintances, and colleagues past, current, and future.

Curiosity can help you figure out whom you want to become as a person and what you wish to do professionally. By not closing the door to options, you can find your way much more readily.

Anticipating and shaping your professional future is the key to avoiding the need for that ever-elusive, just-in-time, desirable job offer. Alternatives rarely surface on their own when you most need them. Appealing options most frequently come to those who are in perpetual motion and who are driven to realize their dreams.

Opportunities arise for those who perform superbly at their current job, activate their Rolodexes, and remain intellectually restless and socially engaged.

Here is a concise summary of the signposts anyone searching for meaningful work would be wise to follow. Your career journey at first might seem intimidating. Actually, it can be filled with the pleasure of discovery. In overcoming obstacles and easing the way to identifying and securing meaningful work, you will learn much about employment opportunities and even more about yourself in relationship to them.

*Start Now* was written to help you, to serve as your Sherpa.

## The Search for Meaningful Work: Guiding Principles

1. It is never too early to prepare for meaningful work. A career is biography in motion.

2. Schools educate. Employers train.

3. What matters most is not the name of the college that offers you admission, but what you do there after enrolling.

4. The absolute worst time to look for a job is when you need one.

5. The more you accumulate knowledge, experience, skills, and responsibility, the greater the likelihood of success.

6. Desirable work is out there. What you can bring to it comes from the qualities of mind and character that you nurture. Pay attention to both the external and internal dimensions of the hunt for professional satisfaction.

7. Build a network of active relationships. Securing meaningful work and succeeding professionally is a collective enterprise.

8. In life's pursuits, always aim to be "in the room where it happens." Serendipity often prevails over planning.

9. In the quest for that dream job, hustle eats strategy for breakfast.

10. In considering where your passion, experience, and abilities might take you, "This above all: to thine own self be true."

11. Few decisions are more important to your professional future than those related to the quality of your life at home.

12. Energy, enthusiasm, curiosity, intelligence, humility, likability, and a secure sense of self are vital traits in a candidate. Tend to them.

13. Finding meaningful work is not a hobby or an extracurricular activity. Research, reflection, and deliberate practice are indispensable to success.

14. In deciding where to compete for meaningful employment, seek a direct supervisor who can serve as a willing mentor in an organizational culture compatible with your values and operating style.

15. Friends, colleagues, and acquaintances acquired throughout life can be indispensable allies in your search for that significant job. Many are willing to help. But only if you overcome the hesitancy to ask.

16. Prepare for a job interview so well that it becomes more of a conversation than an interrogation.

17. You have competed successfully. The job offer is yours for the taking. Now, pause, for the table has turned. Do you really want this post? Should you accept it? And, if so, on what terms?

# Start Now

### Because the Best Time to Look for a New Job
### Is When You Are Securely Settled in Another One

---

Conversely, the absolute worst time to look for a job is when you are unemployed and need one.

If you are in the market for a change of employment, take comfort from the company you are keeping. American workers are on the move, changing jobs very often. Even more give serious thought to doing so but decide to stay longer in their current position while continuing to look around.

Experiencing frequent mobility at work is almost always stressful and disconcerting. Being unemployed can be frightening. It matters not whether you resigned or were dismissed from your last post, whether you are entering the job market for the first time or looking for a position in a new city where you have moved to follow a domestic partner. Competing to fill an available opening is often a jarring, difficult process to manage.

Beginning fresh or starting over is rarely easy. Finding potential desirable employers, gaining access to them, and persuading one— just one—of your worth is challenging and humbling.

These transitional situations, among others, like midlife crisis or career stall, have been described to me by hundreds of nervous adults asking for advice.

It is never too early to prevent such a crisis from developing or enduring.

When you ask admired professionals how they were first hired, common themes emerge. They were lucky to find themselves in a position to take advantage of an unexpected opportunity. Someone they knew, often not for long, offers them a chance, or responds favorably to a request for help.

The high school student who worked as a golf caddy may be assisted by one of the club members. An intern at a newspaper who reviewed websites, fetched coffee, and conducted some occasional research might suddenly be asked to track down a crime story, substituting for a beat reporter who took ill. An earnest and hardworking student at a public elementary school on the south side of Chicago is encouraged by a teacher to apply to a prestigious private school and become the first member in his family to attend college. A part-time intern drafting answers to customer mail and online inquiries is asked to take a full-time post as a staff vacancy suddenly emerges. The elected or appointed official needs a staffer willing to devote every waking hour to a reelection effort, or to prepare for a high-stakes congressional hearing, or to draft a pivotal speech. She, of much talent, who believes that sleep is overrated, often fills the desirable vacancy.[1]

Get ready. Broaden your life experience. Consider some of these options.

Travel. Apprenticeships. Deferred admission to college or graduate school in order to work or volunteer, otherwise referred to as taking a gap year. Part-time voluntary service. Accepting gig or freelance work and pro bono assignments. Reading, widely and deeply. Meeting new people and intentionally broadening your social and professional network. These are experiences that open minds to new occupational ideas and that open doors to their successful pursuit.

That summer job as a lifeguard. Your fellow parishioners at church or congregants at synagogue. The basketball league or chorus or book club or community center you have joined. The co-op board, the tenants' committee, the neighborhood preservation group or friends and colleagues of your parents. Every day you encounter those who can help you. Pause. Establish relationships and connections in these settings and offer others your assistance, expressing interest in their favorite ideas and causes.

Conquer your reluctance to ask for a favor. Like an introduction to a potential employer. Like placing a favorable phone call praising you. People who know and like you are generally eager to help. Render it as easy as possible for them to do so by being specific and providing all they need to honor your request. You will be pleasantly surprised at the number of allies who come to your side. But not unless you explicitly request detailed help.

When an experienced and influential person agrees to converse about your future, take full advantage of the opportunity for that informational interview.

Come prepared for the encounter. Develop questions that connect the background of your meeting partner to the field(s) of greatest interest to you.

Take notes. Listen attentively. Don't come across as casual. Arriving at the orientation session with specific ideas in mind will help you determine how best to follow up. It will furnish natural reasons to keep in touch with each of your informal advisers.

For example, be sure to report back to them so as to reinforce the relationship. "Yes, I read that book you recommended. Yes, I took your advice and contacted that former client/partner/colleague of yours. It was an extremely valuable encounter. And, by the way, I hope you will not mind my circling back to you to report on my progress in the weeks ahead."

This kind of continuing contact helps to keep you on the minds of those who are well connected in the employment marketplace. It suggests that you are interested in developing a relationship and not just engaging in a transaction. It contributes to building a coterie of associations that accumulate over time, advancing your career and enriching your life.

## Look Around, Purposefully

Think of yourself as devoted to, but not defined by, the position you currently hold. Some believe that if you perform well at your current job, the future will take care of itself. Maybe. Even if you are a highly regarded employee, always keep open to new ideas and to playing different roles. Thinking about other possibilities then becomes a habit. Being dedicated to success in your current post is important to your employer and to developing a superb track record of performance. But fidelity to where you are now situated professionally should not blind you to a future brimming with other alternatives, inside the current organization that employs you, or elsewhere. Sound advice comes in a two-word package: heads up.

Just as it is far easier for employers to keep able personnel than to constantly recruit, onboard, and train newcomers, so staying in the same firm successfully is generally a more sensible course of action than running the risk of leaving prematurely. If you are in an environment that encourages personal development, learn all that you can and look carefully for promotion or lateral openings that play to your strengths and your capacity to grow.

If you like your employer, do everything you can to exceed expectations and move up before you decide to move out. Ironically, developing a track record of accomplishment where you are now working can also be a critical factor in landing a coveted position elsewhere.

While it is true that recruiters are more accustomed to hiring executives who have shifted from employer to employer with greater frequency, still, the burden of persuasion is on you, the applicant, to explain why an average length of stay in any one place was relatively short. Professional relocations that occur too frequently hardly allow the time for significant on-the-job achievement. Employee butterflies do not leave much of an impression on any single place they may choose to land.

Once you have become very familiar with the routines, expectations, and culture of your current employer, leaving for what appears

to be a greener pasture may be perilous. What is your tolerance for risk, if the new place does not work out? Do you, and those dependent on you, possess the resources, financial and psychological, to rebound from an error in judgment? Generally, such circumstances are favorable for those at the relatively young end of the age spectrum and for those who have already enjoyed a successful career. Whoever falls into either category will tend to feel freer to pursue new and different challenges that involve higher risk.

To assure yourself that a particular change is right for you, homework awaits. Pay attention to the situational setting of your prospective employer, to its assets and liabilities, and, most importantly, to the particulars of the new setting in which you might work. Are you comfortable with the culture of the new environment, with your likely boss and with your possible immediate colleagues? Beyond extensive reading, have you spoken with current and former employees and taken a hard look at the extremely useful website Glassdoor, which records employee views of the organization? Have you asked penetrating questions of the search firm, if one is involved in the hiring process?

There are no one-size-fits-all approaches to employee mobility Still, the younger you are, or the more financially secure, the greate your ability to assume an economic risk. You can afford to absorb setback. In your twenties and early thirties, or after a remunerativ career, you are likely to be more able to jump into a situation wher both opportunity and uncertainty await. The upside of a soun decision may well be greater than the downside of an error in judg ment. In such circumstances, mistakes are more affordable. Th can be viewed as learning opportunities. And potential future er ployers are more forgiving, even admiring, of those not many ye out of college or graduate school and those with accomplished sumés who pursued a dream and took a calculated chance.

All of us benefit from building a reservoir of knowledge ab other kinds of work and other walks of life. Discover what app to you professionally and geographically. Develop preferences

enable you to seize opportunities as they emerge and to resiliently handle disappointments at your current place of employment.

I have encountered hundreds of adults in their thirties and forties or older, who, having been refused a promotion or an increase in responsibility or compensation, correctly conclude that they have reached a dead end. Alas, they often do not have the slightest idea of how to move forward.

Too often, corporate executives, nonprofit managers, and professionals like lawyers, accountants, and consultants have narrowed the scope of their lives. Over time, their network of friends and colleagues shrinks. Their intellectual and social curiosity dwindles. They read and travel less adventurously, if at all. They prefer the barbecue at home, poolside or at the club, to that new restaurant, that compelling piece of theater or travel to destinations outside their comfort zone. They live near their colleagues and worship in the same congregations. Their kids attend the same schools and compete in identical sports. Routines take over their lives.

Families can become more insular, less outgoing. Opportunities to volunteer to serve nonprofit institutions or to participate in civic and political life may be neglected. Then, if advancement at work is blocked or the ax falls, there seems to be no place to turn for advice or guidance, no options to exercise.

Avoid that fate. Instead, keep open to new ideas, people, travel destinations, and cultural experiences. Try that unusual book. Improve your tennis stroke or take up another sport. Don't let a week go by without connecting to friends, acquaintances, or colleagues in allied or entirely different professional fields. Do not let a month pass without meeting someone new whose work is of interest.

This can all be done quite naturally. It can be accomplished deliberately. It can be woven into your monthly schedule of activities. But let's be honest. Building a broad base of knowledge and a wide range of colleagues and friends takes time. It also takes persistence.[2] And it means there will be less time available with family or for simply relaxing.

Standard financial advice encourages investors to diversify the assets in their portfolios. American firms, large, medium, and small, should certainly be considered for investment purposes. So should companies based overseas in developed and emerging markets. And depending on your risk tolerance, investments in other assets like real property, commodities, or private equity and hedge funds might also be considered. Of course, sufficient cash for annual expense needs and to seize market opportunities should be set aside. Investing wisely in different kinds of holdings requires knowledge. Done well, it demands study, reading, and listening carefully to experts with excellent track records.

If all of this is true about how to handle accumulated wealth, why shouldn't it also be valid for the generator of that capital, the ultimate source of those funds—namely, you?

Unless you are an expert in a highly specialized field like artificial intelligence, neuroscience, or brain surgery, and love your work, spreading professional bets and hedging them is a wise course of action. It is highly likely that your employer today will not be the same five years from now. Are you preparing for that change within a given field, in an adjacent area of endeavor, or in an entirely new one?

Do not be complacent. Do not let inertia take hold. Invest in yourself and your future.

Now, I have known men and women who fall in love with their place of employment and cannot imagine working anywhere else.

They are captivated by the organization's mission and purpose. They are gratified that their knowledge and skills are fully utilized. They naturally become long-serving loyalists.

While others in similar circumstances might become bored, they feel challenged and appreciated. Under such conditions, it is no surprise that tenure at one firm or nonprofit or in government can last decades.

But long lengths of stay are increasingly rare. Many in customer-serving outfits—law, consulting, accounting, public relations and lobbying firms—feel frustrated and unsatisfied. Clients can be both demanding and unresponsive. Their needs must be addressed in late evenings, on weekends and on holidays. New associates might find their assignments monotonous and their treatment less than respectful, even demeaning.

The financial advantage of this kind of professional life and its relative stability can be overwhelmed by work that seems unimportant and repetitive, or where the positive impact of an engagement is difficult to discern.

One of the strong motivations for changing professional positions stems from your current state of disappointment. If you are a consultant, a lawyer, or an investment adviser, your guidance may or may not be taken seriously by clients. Even if it is well regarded and thoughtfully considered, your recommendations may not have more than marginal influence. Frequently, you simply do not know.

Others are, by definition, observers, scribes, or analysts. Journalists, media commentators, public intellectuals, and academics, like political scientists, historians, and sociologists, peer through the windows of space and time wondering what being a decision maker is really like.

As with the leading man in the Broadway musical *Dear Evan Hansen*, many professionals feel they are on the "outside, always looking in." They long to move away from reporting, analyzing, supporting, interpreting, or teaching what others do. They aspire to be at the center of the action, protagonists, not analysts, movers and shakers, not hired hands, let alone hired guns.

In serving clients, you are often not invited to sit around the decision table at critical moments. Much like Aaron Burr, in Lin-Manuel Miranda's brilliant musical *Hamilton*, you yearn helplessly to be in "the room where it happens."

Ultimately, you ask yourself whether your work matters and to whom.

To be sure, your clients pay their bills and you may be doing well financially.

But your hopes for more go unrealized, and you notice that the years are passing.

This sense of feeling incomplete, of being held back, is hardly confined to those who serve clients. At one time or another, restlessness and the desire for change is part of almost everyone's professional life experience.

In every post I have held, there came a time when questions about leaving it began to surface. Was I on the threshold of having accomplished most agreed-upon objectives? Had a strong staff and board been built that could carry on if I departed? Was I becoming ready for a new challenging assignment elsewhere?

Several years before I anticipated the change in position, I would intentionally arrange for appointments with a half dozen wise, experienced, and well-connected colleagues and mentors and an equal number of similarly situated VIPs whom I did not know but whom I sought to reach through third parties.

Having secured an audience, I would present myself. In ten minutes or so, I described who I am and what I think I'd accomplished, personally and professionally. Based on this review, I would then ask if there were any fields of interest, institutions, or even specific openings that came to mind for which I was especially qualified. Invariably, my interlocutors asked terrific questions that caused me to think about the future in new and different ways. I began to question long-held assumptions about my own range of interests and capabilities. Without leaving my current post, I explored more actively other possibilities by diversifying my reading, meeting new people, engaging in more consulting, public speaking, teaching, writing, and nonprofit volunteer activity.

There is an adage in fundraising worth remembering: "If what you want is money, then begin by asking for advice." Well, the same holds true when seeking a new job. More often than not, those from whom I sought general counsel kept me in mind as specific openings revealed themselves. Concretely, a few were called to my attention, even though I may never explicitly have asked to be plugged in to job vacancies.

These meetings, informal encounters, and informational interviews allowed me to be an insider in more places, to learn about what it would really be like to work in different cities, to imagine myself playing a variety of different leadership roles. After all, the search for a new job is, in part, a rediscovery of who you are and what you're about. Identities and values change over time. Defining them is neither automatic nor easy. The help of mentors and protégés is invaluable in determining what you wish to be when you grow up. They can be helpful practically as well as conceptually.

Throughout my professional life, there have been positions I mused about. They were products of my imagination and speculation. They were answers to questions like: What if you could do anything? Or, just suppose you were to receive a call offering you that dream job. Who would be on the other end of that telephone?

Here is but one example. I hope it ignites your imagination. The happiest job seekers I know have their heads in the clouds while their feet are planted firmly on the ground. They remain excited by, yet realistic about, the alternative futures it is possible to envision.

## What If, Just Imagine

I was very eager to meet Richard Holbrooke.

His diplomatic stints in Vietnam and as ambassador to Germany were highly regarded. To this day, he remains the only American to have served as the assistant secretary of state for both European and Asian affairs. Richard's accomplishments as a brilliant and driven public servant had been widely admired for years. He enjoyed a well-deserved reputation for getting important things done.

Holbrooke was the last of some seventy-five trustees I was determined to meet one on one either before or immediately after I became president of the International Rescue Committee. What's more, he had just—against all odds—successfully negotiated the Dayton Accords, terminating the Bosnian War. Indeed, the delay in seeing him was caused by his writing a book about that subject entitled *To End a War*.[3]

After Labor Day in 1997, I called him at home to confirm our appointment for later that week.

"Yes, it's on my calendar. I would like to meet you, although you should know I supported another candidate for the job that you now hold as president of the International Rescue Committee."

"I guess that proves that no one is perfect, Richard. But I bring you warm greetings from Vera and Ambassador to Hungary Donald Blinken."

"Yes? What were you doing in Budapest?"

"Vera asked me to officially open an exhibit on Varian Fry [Fry was a volunteer who courageously arranged for several thousand refugees fleeing the Nazis to escape via the port of Marseille or over the Pyrenees Mountains to Portugal and freedom]. My wife and I stayed in the official residence, and Vera and Donald proudly showed us photographs of your marriage to Kati [Kati Marton, an accomplished author, and like Vera Blinken, a Hungarian refugee] on the grounds of the embassy. They were beaming with pride at hosting your marriage."

"Of course they would. So far, our marriage is the highlight of Donald's tenure as ambassador."

Whoa.

That unprompted remark seemed, even for Holbrooke, over-the-top. Dick's reputation for having an oversized ego both preceded and followed him.

Flash forward a half dozen years or so. Hillary Clinton, then a US senator from New York, is staying over the weekend at the lovely Bridgehampton home of our friends Ellen Chesler and Matt Mallow. Following a summer afternoon's fundraiser and a Saturday night dinner party, we had the senator to ourselves for Sunday brunch and a long walk on the beach. I vividly recall Matt asking her this question: "Hillary, what was it like to be the first lady when everyone who entered the White House focused like a laser beam on you and your husband for eight years?"

"Well, not everybody. I can think of one person Bill and I always talked about who conducted himself differently—Dick Holbrooke.

He regularly looked over the president's shoulder and my own to see whether there was someone else more important behind us!"

In view of Dick's impetuousness and air of superiority, why did Secretary of State Hillary Clinton become his staunchest supporter in the Obama administration, while the president himself and others in the White House wished to see Holbrooke sidelined?

Try sheer brilliance. Drive. Tenacity. Indefatigable energy.

Dick served as the ambassador to the United Nations during my tenure at the IRC. What he achieved in a seventeen-month period was simply breathtaking.

Many others had tried, but it was Holbrooke who persuaded Senator Jesse Helms, then the powerful chairman of the Senate Foreign Relations Committee, to allow the United States to finally pay the $1 billion debt that it had accumulated at the United Nations. This source of international embarrassment seemed impossible to favorably resolve until Holbrooke applied his charm, diplomacy, and not a little groveling to achieve a breakthrough. America was no longer the world's biggest deadbeat.

He brought all African heads of state to the United Nations to meet together for the first time. He persuaded Secretary-General Kofi Annan to devote an entire set of Security Council meetings to the subject of detecting and treating what then appeared to be a worldwide epidemic of a disease called AIDS. And he advocated successfully for a change in international law, embodying recognition for the first time that internally displaced people (IDP) who were separated from their homes by armed conflict, or fleeing in fear of persecution, but who had not crossed an international border would be entitled to the same benefits—bilateral and multilateral—as refugees by the traditional definition.

The term *IDP* is now widely accepted in international parlance, and millions of benighted people in that condition who are being helped have Richard Holbrooke, first and foremost, to thank.

What he accomplished was nothing short of miraculous. That is why Hillary was able to laugh off Richard's propensity to look over her husband's shoulder. It is probably why the Blinkens forgave him for his excess. And it is certainly why, when he was alive, were he ever to call and ask for help, I would drop everything and work day and night to advance his agenda.[4]

Even now, I regret that the phone never rang.

That first meeting and subsequent interactions with Holbrooke ignited my imagination about new possibilities for myself, perhaps in the diplomatic service. I was caught up in the energy field he created around him, always sensing opportunities for forward movement on key issues that mattered, often to the most vulnerable, those without a voice, those devoid of influence. His whirlwind of activity richly informed my government relations leadership as president of the International Rescue Committee. That role required lots of negotiation with major officials in nation-states and with multilateral organizations, like the World Bank, the United Nations High Commission for Refugees, and the European Union.

By observing carefully the lives of people you admire and institutions you respect, tantalizing professional options can surface. Never close yourself off from them.

## The Satisfactions and Limitations of Work

More than a few of my friends and acquaintances at some point in their adult lives become bored, listless, or disenchanted with their employer. Tired of the routine built into their working weeks, they long for something different, something more.

Have you ever wondered, "Could this be all there is?"

Do you wish to exercise unused intellectual muscles? Encounter new challenges and people? Yearn for a change of scene, of pace, and of professional challenge? Do you feel that there has to be more to work than providing financially for your family and winning the respect of your colleagues?

These are among the motivations driving those seeking career advice who find their way to me and to other mentors and executive coaches. Sometimes the solution to their anomie is to play a different role for their current employer, or to seek a post elsewhere in the same field, in an adjacent discipline, or in an entirely fresh undertaking.

But often the driving force for changing circumstances at work is a function of excessive or misplaced expectation.

Your working life may offer many sources of satisfaction, but consider what it is unlikely to provide.

It is no replacement for a nurturing and supportive family.

It is not necessarily the best place to cultivate enduring friendships.

It may or may not be where you can contribute to a larger cause or help others who are less fortunate.

Nor is the workplace a substitute for the pleasures of travel, the discoveries awaiting you in the visual and performing arts, the life-long challenge of athletics, and the richness of reading all kinds of literature.

Cultivate talents that are unrelated to work. Nurture hobbies that are gratifying. Join a book club. Fly-fish. Stay in shape.

Spend more purposeful, undistracted time with family. Acquire sports memorabilia, wine, art, or vintage clothing. Learn new skills.

For some, joining a nonprofit board of directors, or a professional association, or an alumni chapter, or a luncheon or country club, offers the opportunity to break out of daily rituals. To meet different people. Encounter new ideas. Combine forces with the likeminded to pursue a dream, solve a problem, strengthen a movement, exercise leadership.

And what about causes outside yourself? How much time do you spend helping others in need of your talents and skills to tackle a political, social, or environmental challenge?

For many, the emptiness and drift attributed to work amounts to an incorrect diagnosis. Missing instead may be sufficient investment of time and energy on family, on personal development, on civic involvement—all activities outside the workplace.

The immense satisfactions that come from helping others, from contributing to causes and issues beyond self, to public service in the broadest sense, has a claim on millions of Americans.

Out there is a nonprofit board of directors governing in a compelling field of interest and needing someone with just your energy, skill, and experience. Out there is an opportunity for service on municipal commissions and community advisory boards. And just as inviting are chances for you to help real people in your community: in soup kitchens, homeless shelters, scout troops, foster care settings, and after-school activities.

Engaging in pursuits that enrich your domestic partner and children, or enhance the self, and/or partaking in a wider world in need of repair is often an elixir for what you mistakenly thought could be fixed at the workplace.

So consider reconfiguring your life to leave more room for personal growth, civic engagement, and social connection. Notice how pleasurable it is to establish new friendships, address issues that matter, and strengthen charitable organizations of consequence. Then determine whether the emptiness that compelled you to dwell on changing jobs remains present or nearly as prominent. It is often the case that such a void has been filled in other ways through methods only tangentially connected to vocation, if at all.

On the other hand, you may be satisfied that these other parts of life are in reasonably good shape and that it is work which has lost meaning, or at least its magnetic attraction. If so, then by all means follow a road map marked by questions that will clarify the kind of place and post you might find appealing.

## The Search for Meaningful Work: Ten Pertinent Questions

1. As you proceed on this journey, who are your fellow travelers? Identify the mentors, advisers, supporters, and others familiar with your work who are interested in your future and willing to help.

2. What elements of employment offer you the most professional satisfaction?

3. In what functional area(s) do you wish to work? Do you intend to build on your experience in finance, development, public relations, marketing, or programming, or are you hoping for a more diversified assignment or an entirely different one?

4. In what fields of interest do you desire to apply these skills? Health? Primary or secondary school education? Colleges and universities? The visual or performing arts? Consumer products? The defense industry? High tech?

5. Where do you wish to work geographically? How mobile are you if opportunities surface outside your home base?

6. Do you prefer working in large, medium, or small organizations?

7. Are you looking for a position that affords a measure of independence, or do you long for collaborative team environments?

8. What are your current salary requirements?

9. Why are you looking for work? What combination of the place you are fleeing from and the one you are gravitating toward motivates your (re)entry into the labor market?

10. Thinking longer term, where would you like to be professionally five and ten years from now?

## "An Ounce of Experience Is Worth a Pound of Logic"[5]

Answers to questions like these provide informed guidance on your search. They construct the equivalent of a Google map for those who feel bewildered by complexity and overwhelmed by how and where to begin. Armed with the directions supplied by the responses to these queries, job seekers can identify specific institutions and look for existing vacancies. It is now possible for you to call upon that network of friends and associates requesting introductions to key employees or trustees at these desirable places of employment. Often, they know which vacancies are likely to emerge or what kind of restructuring plans a new CEO, COO, or department head has in mind.

All of a sudden, the altitude of the search has been lowered and targets of opportunity become more visible.

This approach is practical in the extreme. It flows inductively from any aspirant's values, skills, interests, and marketplace realities. It avoids arid theories and broad planning designs. They often crash-land in the real world of opportunity, sudden market need, serendipity, and good luck. That's been my experience.

Proceeding in this way enables you to activate your network and to focus on a finite number of desirable openings. It releases you from all of the distracting noise in the turbulent employment market. In its place, you are invited to find the signals that lead to tangible opportunity.

I am a fan of *The Axe Files*. I've listened to every one of David Axelrod's three hundred and fifty and counting podcast episodes. He converses with public officials, past and present, journalists, editors, elected and appointed government representatives, and political consultants. I am also a fan of David Rubenstein's *Peer-to-Peer Conversations*, aired on Bloomberg TV, and of his dialogues at the Economic Club of Washington, DC. These have involved over one hundred prominent figures in important corporate, finance, and political positions.

Both men are fascinated by biography and ask their interviewees how they progressed in their careers. I cannot recall a single guest who proceeded in accordance with a preexisting strategic plan or followed an explicit road map. Yet the literature is sprinkled with books and monographs that proceed deductively, in Cartesian fashion. They recommend designing a complex, multifaceted plan. Titles like *The Strategic Career: Let Business Principles Guide You*, *Reinvention Roadmap*, or *Designing Your Life: How to Build a*

*Well-Lived, Joyful Life* are indicative of top-down, systematic grand schemes.[6]

It has become an axiom of military wisdom that "no battle plan survives first contact with the enemy."[7] Similarly, deductive, formulaic directions to acquire a desirable job often crash-land in the stormy conditions of the real world.

My recommendations are based on a completely different premise: that real-life encounters in the marketplace of jobs and ideas are far more valuable than attempting to develop and then follow a theoretical framework for action. I adhere to the view that in the labor market, an ounce of experience *is* worth a pound of logic. Particularly given how quickly employees are moving from place to place, how rapidly the content of jobs is changing, and how markedly what it means to experience a satisfying life differs among adults of varying ages and expectations.

If *Start Now* were therapy, sessions would be short-term, interactive, and pragmatic. No Freudian analysis. No four-day-a-week, multiyear commitments. No psychoanalyst who remains detached and mostly silent, posing conceptual questions but being unwilling to offer practical guidance. For that matter, in these pages, PowerPoint slides and ten-year plans will not be found.

Your network of friends and colleagues might be in a position to offer more than general job-finding advice. Relationships you developed at work, at school, at social and athletic activities, in volunteer assignments, in country or luncheon or book clubs, or in alumni networks, can be matched to the specific target of opportunity you are now pursuing.

Think about your life as a series of personal and professional connections. Over time your challenge is to convert those you have accumulated from a source of interactions to a body of relationships. When your colleagues or associates feel an affinity for you based on positive interaction and the assistance you may have provided them, a willingness to return the favor becomes natural. Such counterparts are often more than willing to help with a persuasive reference, sound advice, or negotiating tips.

At the center of a relationship network, imagine that there is an ATM. For moments like this, when you are pursuing a real opening at a place where you desire to work, it is helpful to have made more deposits than withdrawals into the account of the person whose assistance can be helpful. When you have aided peers and mentors, it will be far more comfortable to ask for a favor of them. The request will come naturally, and it is highly likely to be honored. Turnabout is fair play.

You may wonder how it is possible to provide valuable help to someone decades older, probably much wealthier and certainly far more experienced.

Well, begin with the practical. Can you offer to conduct research, or type a manuscript, or perform an errand or two? Do you remember a birthday, anniversary, or other important event in the life of that mentor?

The accomplished and curious will be keenly interested in your perspectives, in how you see the world and manage your life. Prepare yourself to talk about the way you use technology, what you are reading and streaming, and with whom you are impressed in common fields of interest. Offer to have coffee or breakfast or lunch, just to stay in touch. Be generous with your time but cautious about intruding on the life of your hoped-for confidant.

As my Rolodex yellowed at work, I turned to former and current associates and acquaintances who were considerably younger for recommendations on whom to hire for specific job openings. I'd ask them about the latest trends in fashion and in travel. What restaurants have they found hot in a city filled with choice was always of keen interest to me.

This very book was read and critiqued in manuscript form by several former colleagues, some of whom are forty years younger than I. Their generational perspectives and critiques are invaluable.

These connections are not just a function of good manners. They are substantively meaningful. I am fortunate to enjoy dozens upon dozens of such relationships. They predispose me to jump at the chance to be helpful whenever I am called upon and to offer, unsolicited, advice and guidance.

But if I am only contacted by an erstwhile friend or acquaintance when I am suddenly needed, after many months of silence or years of disengagement, the inclination to respond favorably fades. It is not that I am unwilling. It is that we have lost a vital relationship with one another. We no longer have much in common.

Building a potent network consumes valuable time. It requires frequent communication with colleagues, current and former, associates, friends, and acquaintances. Email, telephone, and face-to-face catch-ups solidify relationships. It is through just such a web of connections that intelligence about job openings can be gathered, as can ideas on how best to attempt to fill them. Summon the energy and determination to meet those whom you can help and who can, in turn, come to your aid.

In doing so, social media, like LinkedIn and Facebook, can be a useful tool to begin a new connection or to locate a former classmate or colleague with whom you have not kept in touch.

This propensity to keep connected to social peers, fellow employees, mentors, and protégés is particularly well suited to readers who are now settled in a post and are thinking about leaving it.

It is also relevant to those in jobs that by their very nature enjoy a limited life: the ballet dancer, the athlete, the police officer, those in the military. These occupations and others like them are filled with gifted professionals who are fully aware that the sand in the hourglass of their job longevity continues to fall. Fear not. There is gainful and satisfying employment after such first careers. These skilled workers and all of those around them—executives, agents, financial advisers—need to develop, or help their clients to think about, new and different interests, or simply playing different roles. The athlete in the broadcast booth. The dancer as choreographer or teacher. Either as authors, stock market analysts, or real estate developers.

What all have in common is that they need to start now. To read, to build relationships, to imagine themselves in different places of work. By enrolling in classes, by acquiring counselors, and by creating a collection of supporters, these short-term professionals will take advantage of the limited duration of their current job and ready themselves for the next one.

But what if you are trying to decide on where to apply for that first job? Stepping farther back in time, what if you are about to enroll in college? And what if you have become a parent or a grandparent mulling over how best and how soon to guide the children for whom you are responsible to a productive, fulfilling life?

These are some of the leading questions preoccupying those who have not yet begun careers in earnest.

As the lyrics of the classic Rodgers and Hammerstein song from *The Sound of Music* instruct, the beginning is a "very good place to start."

# - 3 -

# It's Never Too Early

## (Or Too Late)

---

**M**y wife, Elizabeth, and I are blessed with a granddaughter named Colette. Inadvertently, the initials of her first, middle, and last names spell *CEO*. That moniker suggests what her parents hope she can achieve, if she wishes. In the meantime, this CEO certainly commands the pleasurable attention of her grandparents.

One late afternoon, I was reading to Colette at the end of what had been a long day. She arose at 7 a.m. in order to arrive at pre-kindergarten by 9 a.m. In between, there was the necessary grooming, cleaning, and dressing routines and a breakfast to consume. The 3 p.m. dismissal was followed by an after-school ballet class, a devoured snack, and then the trek from Manhattan to our home in Riverdale, a lovely section of the Bronx just north of the George Washington Bridge. Now, it was 5:30 p.m.

As I began my dramatic reading of *Cloudy with a Chance of Meatballs*, Colette started to yawn. Soon after, so did I.

"Colette, you know, if you yawn, then I will, and we will never finish this story."

"I know, Reynold. Yawning is contagious."

Where did this four-year-old learn the meaning of the word *contagious*? Its use engendered a conversation between us about what else besides yawning could spread so quickly from person to person. A cold? A fever? What is an infection, anyway? And how can we ward it off?

Before you could snap your fingers, Colette and I were animatedly discussing diet, exercise, sleep, washing of hands, and other behavior conducive to health.

## The Formative Years

What combination of genetics and the environment allows students to flourish in school and professionally? How much should we attribute to nature and how much to nurture?

Valued at the workplace are not only capabilities, aptitudes, and native intelligence, but desirable personality traits and habits.

Curiosity, energy, a sense of humor, modesty, determination, the propensity for teamwork, a willingness to extend yourself for the organization and the mission beyond the narrowly drawn boundaries of any particular job. These sought-after characteristics when paired with problem-solving skill and the constant willingness to learn are what employers highly value.

One fundamental lesson of the psychological and pedagogical literature is that both the cognitive and the intuitive, the ability to reason and the personality that embodies it, are formed at an extremely young age.[1]

The search for life's meaning and for meaningful work really begins at birth. It is then that sensitivity to stimuli commences. It is then that curiosity awakens. It is then that the human potential to learn is either encouraged by adults or languishes for want of attention. It is then that enduring relationships begin to form. From birth until age six or so, the cerebrum is at its most elastic and able to convert adult and peer prompting to embedded memory with relative ease.

Transforming sounds into words. Moving from crawling to standing to walking. Recognizing shapes and colors, liquids and solids, hot and cold. Acquiring trust in selected adults. These are the building blocks of early learning. So much of what we accomplish later in life can be attributed to the stimulation and guidance of adults in baby to toddler to preschool years.

Did your parents talk to you? Read to you? Play with you?

Did they arrange opportunities for you to mix and mingle with peers? Did they take you on trips to the park, to the museum, to the playground? Did they organize playdates with your friends? Did they have you visit relatives? Did they bring you with them to their workplace and show and tell what Mommy and/or Daddy do for a living?

Were they energetic in exposing you to the zoo and the public library, to sports, arts and crafts, music, and games? It is from such preschool activities and active engagement with peers and adults that the early stirrings of empathy, sharing, teamwork, autonomy, kindness, and self-confidence are born.

If you are or hope to become a parent, will you engage your children in these ways? If a grandparent, you are now blessed with a second chance, this time as a team member, to help raise kids that you, in a way, can call your own. Little will be more important to a child's future, emotionally and cognitively. Because a pleasant disposition, alertness, an elastic attention span, deferred gratification, and a positive sense of self are qualities best learned in the earliest years, even in preschool.

How much time adults, particularly parents and grandparents, spend with infants and toddlers reading, conversing, and being caught up in play really matters.

Emphasis on taking fullest advantage of engagement with a child during the earliest of years is beginning to take hold not only in the literature, but in parental understanding and appreciation. Free universal pre-K classes, in some cities beginning at as early as three years of age, are spreading around the country. This development is in addition to Head Start. As of 2019, the nation's largest preschool program, begun in 1965 as part of President Lyndon Johnson's War on Poverty, enjoyed a $10 billion annual budget and served about nine hundred thousand low-income preschoolers.[2]

Projects are underway to ensure that books are available where all children, particularly poor kids, might congregate. The local public library, of course. But also the pediatrician's office. The playground. The park. The Laundromat. And guidance is being offered to parents who often feel that there is very little time to interact with a baby in the family when there are several other kids to care for, or when a single mother or father also holds a full-time job, one that could involve an unpredictable work schedule.

Research in early childhood development suggests that parents and caregivers can integrate conversing with and singing to kids while handling compulsory tasks.

Take a chore as basic as diaper changing. At an average of eight per day, most parents and caregivers will engage in this task 8,760 times. Since each change takes no less than three minutes, a parent or another caregiver will spend a minimum of 35,240 minutes—or twenty-six full days—changing a child's diaper over the course of three years.[3] And how about the considerable time you will spend at meals or at bedtime, or bathing, with your kids.

So take advantage of these extraordinary face-to-face opportunities by talking to your children, reading to them, and telling them your own stories. Singing and game playing (e.g., peekaboo, true or false, twenty questions) are also conducive to linguistic and cognitive development. These precious intervals in the lives of children and parents are frequent, and they are predictable. Viewing them as learning and bonding opportunities can help to instill self-control, persistence, grit, language acquisition, curiosity, self-confidence, and a sense of security. This combination of cognitive skills and desirable personality traits can be acquired very early in life.

From birth to six years of age is prime time for brain development and character formation. The active involvement of caring adults in a child's earliest years, along with schooling that sets high standards and expectations, often does much to explain adult success at work and in life.

## Work-Life Balance

Precisely because domesticity, including a partner and children, may be in your plans, practically everyone strives to achieve a semblance of balance between success at work and contentment at home.

There are many ways to think about how and when to accomplish both objectives. Virtually impossible is securing that balance all of the time. The demands of the workplace and the sudden opportunity to advance often come at inconvenient intervals in your private life. Employer expectations and the important needs of a companion, children, and other family members rarely coincide fully.

Maintaining that work-life balance is heavily influenced by economic circumstances. If parents can afford after-school classes for their children, retaining a full- or part-time nanny or au pair, as well as babysitters, managing the needs of home and work become a lot easier. Parents who can take vacations, allowing them to reinforce bonds with each other and their children, are very fortunate. So are those, like my daughter, whose relatives are available to pitch in with youngsters in need of supervision.

Even under such circumstances, the surprises of sudden deadlines at work, illness at home, unanticipated travel requirements, and lack of sleep create tensions that are tough to resolve.

Now, consider the single parent who in order to make ends meet needs to work at two jobs. Think about the couple whose work schedules are irregular, or who have minimal, if any, health insurance. Identify with the adult forced to depend on the kindness of strangers to care for a young child at home or compelled to use the emergency room at a hospital as the functional equivalent of the family doctor.

For such poor or working-class adults laboring at or near minimum wage with skimpy benefits, the real challenges to those in higher income brackets seem much more manageable.

No matter the financial situation, communication with your partner at home, or your support team of relatives and friends, is

critical. It may be that your chance for promotion or for that desirable but demanding job change can come at a time consistent with
your husband's, wife's, or companion's availability to carry a larger
share of responsibilities at home. Then, later on, positions can shift
when you enjoy a greater measure of workplace flexibility. Conversing regularly and honestly about personal preferences and about
burden sharing can free both parties to satisfy their needs.

Inevitably, one or the other will sacrifice professional accomplishment for the sake of a partner seizing a workplace opportunity.
Deferred gratification, adjusting to geographic moves and managing a disproportionate share of childcare are just a few of the likely
sacrifices. If the partner taking on more household chores maintains an interest in pursuing his or her career climb, then clarity
about when responsibilities can shift is very important. The same
observation applies to the companion who wishes to pursue a college or graduate school degree, full- or part-time.

There is simply no substitute for an empathic, supportive partner. Strong friendships are very valuable as well. Stability and happiness in your personal life is a fundamental building block for
applying energy, focus, and creativity at work.

Fortunately, Americans today enjoy a longevity ten to fifteen
years longer than they did as late as the 1950s. The acceptance of
adults working longer, often into their seventies, affords a greater
degree of flexibility as to who assumes which responsibilities when
at home.

For some, happiness may not coincide with always "having it
all." Those early, precious years of childhood may find both adults
yearning for more time devoted to parenting. For them, if that
means passing on a taxing assignment at work, or delaying a move
to a different physical location, then so be it.

Childbearing and child-rearing are prominent issues for
many mothers (and some dads, although arguably not nearly
enough of them) who wish to stay at home for a few years and
then re-enter the workforce. Savvy employers who desire to retain
high-performing employees will try to accommodate those who

request an interruption in the continuity of their service. Doing so demonstrates enlightened flexibility and adaptability. It sends a powerful message of appreciation for employee parental choice. It offers peace of mind to the new mom or dad, assuring that there will be an appropriate position reserved at a familiar workplace when either is ready to occupy it.

Many employers cannot or will not provide this kind of accommodation. Then what? Aspiring returnees who are new parents need to keep informed about the job market. Staying close to those actively employed in it allows you to remain up-to-date, even as you nurture loved ones. Definitely read widely in fields of interest and arrange conversations with those you know who are consummate networkers and gatekeepers.

Put differently, you can integrate your commitment to family with your desire to return to professional life. All or nothing, at home or at work exclusively, is not a formula for balance over time. If possible, seek out short-term assignments, or consulting roles at your former employer or at other attractive firms. Building into your weekly schedule the time for job-relevant conversations, events, occasions, reading, and gig-like work need not be inconsistent with taking care of, and deriving pleasure from, a growing family.

Too often, the question of time off and returning to the workplace is put in terms of either/or. For the energetic, industrious, and determined, that is a false choice.

Balance can be thought of in another way. One partner may long to work in the nonprofit sector, pursuing a socially important goal at the expense of enjoying a higher salary. Meanwhile, the other can pursue a more lucrative career, say, in real estate or law, or in investment banking. More than a few of those who worked with me at the International Rescue Committee and Lincoln Center derived great satisfaction from their mission-centered work. Meanwhile, their spouse or companion enjoyed the financial benefits of a position in business.

Not infrequently, a well-trained and well-educated associate who started a career in the Third Sector switched roles with her companion to flex commercial muscles. Staff close to me gravitated to The Walt Disney Company, to private equity, to hedge funds, and to a variety of start-ups. Their partners either stayed with their lucrative roles or decided on a vocational change to begin laboring in nonprofit vineyards like the Tate Museum in London, or the Perot Museum in Dallas, or heading up a local business improvement district in Brooklyn.

The idea that you can have it all and do it all, at any given time, is highly unrealistic. But over the years, mutually supportive adults can accommodate their career needs and the requirements of a content home life.

## The Enduring Importance of College

Where is it written that schools are to be the training ground for America's corporations, small businesses, and firms?

Of course, purely vocational institutes are intended to provide skilled workers to needy employers. Welders. Plumbers. Coders. Automobile and airplane technicians. Construction workers. All who hold such jobs could benefit from a college education, and some will enroll later in life. But matriculating at a community college or four-year school is often not a necessary requirement for such positions. The same observation can apply to dental technicians, elements of nursing and home care, salespeople, and junior administrators of all kinds. Chefs and their assistants, those who wait on tables or take reservations, bank tellers, flight attendants, telephone operators, travel and real estate agents, and hotel and resort management personnel all can perform well without having completed a college education. And that is also true for freelance bloggers, gamers, web designers, copywriters, and childcare workers, among other jobs.

For them, the linkage between for-profit or nonprofit training centers and filling jobs can be tight. Track records of successful placements should be measured accordingly. After all, the whole purpose of these instructional outfits is to prepare students for to-day's jobs, to supply the skills necessary for graduates to succeed in them.

The same rationale can be advanced for undergraduate programs in business, engineering, education, computer science, and design. College students, in significant numbers, major in these fields hoping to secure entry-level jobs immediately after graduation. For them, whether to pursue a graduate degree is a decision that can be reached more intelligently after gaining some experience in the workplace.

But when we move from most blue-collar and some white-collar openings to many entry-level and middle-management positions, expectations shift. The relationship between academics and earning a living is less straightforward. Cause and effect is harder to trace with any level of confidence.

Here's why.

Colleges and universities educate. Employers train. That's the real division of labor. It is sometimes observed that a sound liberal arts education prepares you for everything but trains you for nothing. That focus of the liberal arts college on what it does best works well for both employees and those who pay them. The expectation that most four-year schools prepare students for particular jobs is badly misplaced. It is extremely unrealistic.

Few college faculty or administrators, almost by definition, are closely connected to the general employment marketplace. They left it long ago or never even entered it, preferring an academic life. They are therefore unfamiliar with the swiftly changing needs of "real-world" positions. Even assuming otherwise, they would not know how to adjust the content of college course work to properly train students for the here and now of a hurly-burly employment marketplace. It is not for nothing that those who labor in college and university settings are said to dwell in an ivory tower.

All of the efforts to figure out how much students of different four-year schools earn after graduation, attributing material differences to the source of their education, are fatuous. Ivory towers are not preparation centers for the nation's employers.

Criticisms that liberal arts colleges fare poorly in enabling their students to engage in meaningful work are often misplaced. A phalanx of scholars and journalists has persuasively rebutted them.[4]

The first part of their critique is addressed to what virtually all employers highly value and what faculty and administrators at good liberal arts colleges can deliver.

- How to write and speak clearly, persuasively, and compellingly.

- How to reason through an argument to distinguish between mere assertion and fact.

- How to learn, to acquire knowledge.

- How to work closely with others on team projects.

- How to become conversant with the classics of literature, history, philosophy, and/or social science (political science, economics, psychology, sociology).

- How to analyze a text and to decipher meaning from the written word.

- How to become fluent in foreign languages.

- How to value reading and to dissect arguments, evidence, and ideas.

- How to ask intelligent, penetrating questions.

- How to deliver a paper, or prepare a take-home exam, or respond to a professor's questions, under pressure and on time.

All of these and other acquired skills cannot be nurtured in a setting that consists of large classes with eighty or more students.

They cannot be cultivated by fledgling, harried, and grossly un-derpaid graduate student instructors playing the role of teaching assistants while pursuing their own advanced degrees. The quality of what they can offer students is severely constrained by a lack of knowledge, classroom experience, and adequate time to prepare for teaching, or to offer guidance to enrollees.[5] Nor can needed abili-ties and skills be nurtured for students in online classes, let alone in for-profit diploma mills.

At many of America's colleges and universities, students are still endeavoring to transcribe what the instructor in front of a lecture hall is spouting. As the telling quip goes, too often the notes of the professor become the notes of the student without passing through the mind of either. That observation is unfortunately what passes for education in too many of our country's lecture halls.

Needed skills and useful knowledge are best acquired in small classes, study groups, and other forms of real and sustained student-faculty interaction. Otherwise, opportunities for genuine learning plummet. Rote memorization displaces thinking. The chances for intellectual growth activated by the leader in the class-room or by fellow students all but disappear.

Higher education in America has become big business. It is overwhelmed by administrators and by concerns unrelated to the essence of the college experience: teaching and learning. The ex-pansion of lavish athletic facilities, student centers, and fancy living quarters. The upscale dining options. The numbers of staff suppos-edly devoted to compliance with applicable laws and regulations. When excessive resources are spent on such activities, they are tell-tale signs of what a school really values.

Fareed Zakaria writes in *In Defense of a Liberal Education* that "many large universities have become multi-million-dollar sports franchises with small educational institutions attached to them."[6]

Socrates had no director of housing, no equal opportunity em-ployment administrator, no government relations czar, no admis-sions and financial aid staff. Today, these and other educational and sports bureaucrats vie to outnumber faculty engaged in sustained student instruction.

It is graduates or dropouts from such schools, private and state sponsored, that employers find deficient.

So, in your own search for a college or university, find one that treasures the heart of the enterprise and seeks to protect it. Favor faculty-student ratios that allow for regular interaction between professor and student. Track down a curriculum that demands disciplined and rigorous study. Spot opportunities for students to relate closely with instructors and with one another outside the formal classroom setting.

Even in very large universities, you can find pockets of learning opportunity and enclaves of peer interaction that are intellectually satisfying. Seek out the brightest minds and the most engaging environments. And refrain from majoring too early in one subject area, unless you are really sure of what you wish to learn and why. For most of us, taking advantage of the extensive intellectual treasures you can sample in school before selecting a major is the preferred course of action.

The second line of defense for the continuing vitality of liberal arts colleges flows from the data. For example, it is widely believed that science and business majors earn far more over a lifetime of work than those who study the humanities and social sciences.

In fact, in the decades after graduation, on average, those graduating with comparable grades in the liberal arts differ only modestly in compensation from their business and science counterparts.[7]

It turns out that the key variables for success in the workplace are *not* the employment-specific skills acquired in college, but the ability to learn on the job, the capacity to work productively with others, the ability to communicate well orally and in writing, and the discipline to deliver high-quality work products. Those kinds of qualities and a can-do, team-oriented attitude lead to upward career mobility and financial rewards.

Unless you are passionate about a subject that becomes your major area of study, choose your classes based on the quality of the professors and the students you admire who are drawn to them. And do not neglect study abroad opportunities. Adjusting to life in a different culture and becoming fluent in a foreign language demonstrate receptivity to change and adaptability to an entirely new environment. These very qualities are conducive to highly regarded flexibility in employee behavior and in the proclivity for teamwork.

There is yet another important theme undergirding the linkage between school and work. One important measure of a college's standing is the loyalty of its graduates. For schools that establish a lifelong influence on their students, such devotion is palpable. If you are proud enough of your alma mater to hope that your children will qualify for admission, then it is likely you have become part of a community that regularly and naturally supports graduates.

The networks of dozens of schools across the country that open doors to employers for former students by virtue of the connections of their graduates are strong and powerful. I earned my bachelor's degree at Hobart College. The undergraduate education I enjoyed was simply outstanding. But, with rare exceptions, the faculty and alumni were not in a position or motivated to help students compete for internships, summer jobs, or entry-level posts.

As I served as the CEO of the 92nd Street Y, the International Rescue Committee, the AT&T Foundation, Lincoln Center, and the Robin Hood Foundation, I witnessed the amazing connectivity between and among the alumni of such schools as Stanford, Duke, Brown, Harvard, Princeton, and Howard Universities; Middlebury, Haverford, Amherst, and Spelman Colleges; and the Universities of Michigan, Wisconsin, and Virginia, to name just a few. Their alums would seemingly drop everything to advocate for current students' interests and needs.

I was frequently on the receiving end of calls from donors, trustees, and colleagues importuning me to initiate a hiring process on behalf of one or another graduate, or to favor a competitive candidate. The energy and commitment generated by the common bond of former students at some colleges and universities, even across decades, is very impressive. It manifests itself in internships, apprenticeships, structured gap years, and mentorships. It results in summer jobs, training opportunities, and special project assignments.

So these are the correct ways to think about the connection between school and work. It is not about whether one or another college will prepare you for a particular job or place of employment. It is rather about whether you will graduate with the skills, abilities, aptitudes, motivation, and professional qualities that employers highly value. It is about learning how to think, how to speak your mind well, how to write clearly and compellingly, and how to solve problems on your own and as part of a team. It is about broadening yourself by reading widely, by encountering music, art, and science energetically, and by listening carefully.

And it is about whether the school that fostered these capabilities and instilled the love of learning can do more. Can it, principally through the alumni network, help you identify and land that first job and others to follow throughout the course of your career?

Marc Tessier-Lavigne, a distinguished neuroscientist, was recently appointed president of Stanford University. In 2016 he spoke out on these matters during his inaugural address. He decried the emphasis from parents of college students and politicians on science, technology, engineering, and math. He argued that "the most important skills that could be imparted to undergraduate students are critical and moral reasoning, creative expression, and appreciation of diversity."[8]

For Tessier-Lavigne, "liberal education" meant liberating the mind and resisting a vocational focus. Breadth of learning is what students need most as undergraduates. There will be time enough for specialized study later. This defense of the liberal arts emanated from the former president of Rockefeller University and a senior executive at Genentech.

When weighing his arguments, consider the source.

Or, reflect on Mount Sinai's medical school admission requirements. It will only accept undergraduates who majored in the humanities or the social sciences for one large segment of students.

Premed enrollees at the undergraduate level are strongly discouraged from applying. The MCAT (Medical College Admission Test) is neither necessary to take nor viewed as particularly helpful in predicting the success of medical school students, or of graduates as they practice their profession.

Mount Sinai is looking for medical doctors of intellectual breadth. Future physicians who listen carefully to patients and weigh the ethical and societal implications of their work are highly valued. There is time enough to be trained in the sciences and to develop technical skills expected of medical professionals. That is what Mount Sinai offers.

Like Stanford, Mount Sinai opts for broad exposure to the liberal arts in many of the students it rigorously trains.

And while we turn to academics for advice, heed Professor of Economics Alan B. Krueger. Recently deceased, he beseeched students and parents to stop obsessing about winning the competition to be admitted to the most sought-after college.

> Don't believe that the only school worth attending is the one that would not admit you.
>
> Recognize that your own motivation, ambition, and talents will determine your success more than the college name on your diploma.[9]

Or, to put the matter most succinctly, notice the title of Frank Bruni's bestseller *Where You Go Is Not Who You'll Be: An Antidote to the College Admissions Mania.* What you can do with what you have learned matters most to your success, as do soft skills, according to Bruni's *New York Times* colleague Tom Friedman: "Leadership, humility, collaboration, adaptability and learning and loving to learn and re-learn."

While it is never too early to learn and grow, it is also never too late.

The inevitable intensification of globalization and the advent of applied technology calls for confident worker adaptation. Machine learning, artificial intelligence, driverless cars and trucks, and the spread of robots, among other developments, call for learning new subject matter and acquiring new skills.

Friedman quotes the future-of-work strategist Heather Mc-Gowan on the implications of the blazingly swift change in the workplace.

> The old model of work was three life blocks: Get an education. Use it. And then retire after forty years.
>
> We then made the faulty assumption that the next new model would be: Get an education. Use it for twenty years. Then get retrained. Then use that for twenty more years. And then retire.

But with the acceleration of change in the workplace "the fastest growing companies and the most resilient workers will be those who learn faster than their competition."[10]

## To Be or Not to Be a Graduate Student

Another critical decision point for young and maturing adults relates to formal education beyond college. To enroll or not to enroll, and when, that is the question. "Should I pursue an advanced degree right away or wait, and, if the latter, for how long?"

My answer is straightforward and unequivocal. Test your intellectual interests and skills in real jobs before deciding whether graduate school of any kind is a sensible investment of time and money. When in doubt, wait.

This advice is hard earned. Dispensing it does not come naturally. For I proceeded in exactly the opposite way. Having graduated from Hobart College, I moved directly to acquire a PhD and a law degree over the next seven years. During that prolonged period of reading and study, papers and exams, preparing a master's thesis, defending a doctoral dissertation and modifying it for publication as a book on American foreign policy,[11] I worked many odd jobs. The night shift at a hotel. An airline ticket clerk. A professor's research assistant. A tutor of students. A fraternity chaperone. A taxi driver. The director of summer camps for children and after-school programs for teenagers. These and other ways to earn money plus scholarships and loans financed my continuous, unbroken run of graduate and legal study with no particular vocational end in mind.

I knew what I wanted to learn. I had little idea of how I would earn a living. And I felt even less sure about the connection between the two—learning and earning.

True, I emerged with an intellectual framework in many areas of the humanities, the social sciences, and the law. I left my studies confident about my ability to speak compellingly, write persuasively, and reason clearly. My broad and deep education allowed me to wander through ideas, to grapple with critical questions, to exhilarate in learning, and to relish independence and solitude.

But at twenty-eight years of age, with a freshly minted PhD from the University of Virginia and a law degree from Columbia University, I still had not the slightest notion of what I would do to collect a paycheck. By contrast, most of my counterpart Hobart College graduates had spent seven years from 1966 to 1973 testing their mettle in full-time employment, some with the same employer, others in multiple settings.

To all who ask, I strongly recommend against prolonged, unbroken years of study after college. I counsel against plunging into graduate school immediately. Unless you are certain that astrophysics, brain surgery, architecture, or other such specialties are your passion, please defer enrolling in an advanced degree program.

Instead, acquire on-the-job experience in professional fields to which you are drawn. As you learn from bosses, peers, and mentors, as you spread your wings in the workplace, you will be on a much better path to determine whether more years at work tackling problems and seizing challenges is preferable to enrolling in graduate school. During my teaching years at the Harvard Business School, the most valuable student contributions tended to come from those who had acquired significant work experience before returning to full-time study.

It takes time to decide what really motivates you at work and how you wish to spend most of your waking hours. Closely observing others, conversing directly with professionals engaged in occupations you are considering, and reading about how people like you react to their circumstances at work can be helpful.

But there is no substitute for being thrust into a variety of business, nonprofit, or governmental situations and learning to manage your way through them. What you do well, what you enjoy, is far more likely to become clear as you encounter concrete problems and challenges. When you are no longer role-playing or imagining what could be, but instead are assigned real responsibilities and held accountable for discharging them, perspectives can suddenly change. There is a limit to which abstract reasoning, distance learning, and online education can clue you in to what turns you on.

## The Whys and Wherefores of Sales

Since determining what you might wish to do for a living can itself be a major challenge, let's consider a specific line of work. It is one of many that college graduates can flourish in pursuing with only humanities or social science majors to their credit.

Sales. Yes, sales. Just one of the alternatives that might well appeal to you. Even strictly interpreted, the US economy employs thirteen million people in sales, contrasted to four million, for example, in computer-related jobs.[12]

Now, attach that process of persuasion to a field or an organization you care, or are knowledgeable, about. Commercial real estate. Insurance: life, health, or collectibles. Homes. Cars. Stocks, bonds, and other financial investments. Retail sales, in person or online. Travel. Positions in food and beverage, restaurants and catering.

Let's expand the commonly used label "sales" ever so slightly. Fund-raising, for nonprofits in the form of donations, or for start-ups, venture capital, or private equity firms, in the form of investors. Tickets—to sports, performing or visual arts, pop concerts, or charitable events. Admissions—to private elementary or secondary school, colleges and universities, hospitals and nursing homes. Clients—for law firms, lobbying outfits, advertising, marketing and public relations organizations.

The possibilities abound. Simply put, sales is by far the single largest function in business. It is virtually recession-proof. The barriers to entry are low. The compensation for star performers is impressively high. Importantly, the invaluable opportunity to learn about yourself as you try to convince others what is good for them can hardly be improved upon. Nor can the contribution being involved in the sales process offers to such valuable characteristics as resilience, fortitude, and handling rejection as prospects decline your offers.

Solicitor to donor. Coach to athlete. Teacher to student. Mentor to protégé. Fundraiser to investor. Master to apprentice. Writer to reader. Actor, musician, or dancer to casting director. The first part of all of these couplets is engaged in a dimension of inducing, convincing, influencing, persuading. These are close relatives of sales. Each is selling a cause, an idea, a technique, a discipline, an exercise, or a way of functioning in a field of interest. That is what all of these roles have in common.

And that's part of what attracts me to sales. It is an activity that demands that you listen attentively, communicate compellingly, handle setbacks gracefully, identify with your prospects creatively, and constantly learn more about what you are attempting to sell and about yourself.

Another appealing dimension of sales is that it can transcend a mere job title. It is a portable skill. Sales can be a vital part of the package of capabilities you bring to any enterprise.

Isn't the politician a quintessential salesman? Doesn't a chief executive need to sell a narrative to donors/investors, the media, partners, suppliers, employees, and a governing body of directors or trustees, among others? Journalists sell their story ideas to editors. Sommeliers sell their finest bottles to high-end diners. Auction houses and art dealers sell their precious inventory to collectors and investors.

## My Sales Role Model

When I was seven years old, my father would invite me to sit next to him on the living room couch and watch a daytime program called *Art Linkletter's House Party*. Then a very popular television host and raconteur whose show ran from 1952 to 1969 on CBS, Linkletter devoted a regular segment of his program to audience participation. He'd point to one of its members and invite the guest onto the stage. Then, he'd place a white page telephone directory in front of the "volunteer." Eyes closed, the contestant would be asked to point to any listing.

Linkletter would request that the audience member dial that name and number and tell a brief story to whoever answered the phone. Something like, "Madam, you could win a new washing machine and dryer as a prize if you answer correctly just two questions about any one of three subjects. It will be your choice. Want to play?" The object of the game was to have the caller keep the respondent on the phone for at least three consecutive minutes. A highly visible countdown clock was displayed for all to see in the studio audience and for those watching on television.

Well, it was rare, extremely rare, when any contestant could manage a conversation with that stranger for more than the prescribed time span.

When the show concluded, my dad would hand me our home copy of the white pages and ask me to close my eyes and point to any name and phone number. He would then proceed to dial it and use about the same script as we had just witnessed with whoever answered the phone. Meanwhile, I fixed my gaze on our kitchen clock's second hand, watching it tick away.

I couldn't believe my ears and eyes. Nine out of ten times, Milton Levy won the game, often keeping the conversation flowing for five to ten minutes! Later in life I learned that my father was engaged in cold calling, trying to interest a stranger, out of the blue, in a product or service. Sales veterans will tell you that there is nothing more difficult.

What was Milton's secret?

He didn't focus on the quiz question. He concentrated on whoever had answered his telephone call.

"Good afternoon. I'm Milton Levy. What's your name? I'm sorry to interrupt your day or that of your family. How are you? By the way, do you have a spouse and kids? What are their names and ages? And how is the weather in Queens? You are lucky. It's really cold and bitter in Brighton Beach, Brooklyn. I live only one block from the Atlantic Ocean, and the wind is whipping through our neighborhood at forty miles per hour."

Put simply, Dad expressed genuine interest in the party to whom he was speaking. He didn't hesitate to disclose background information about himself, even as he asked after facts regarding his telephone partner. All of this occurred well before Dad ever reached the potential prize-winning quiz question.

To be sure, these conversations took place decades ago. They preceded such practices and inventions as robocalls, caller ID, sophisticated telephone scams, or even unlisted numbers.

The lessons I learned from these weekly exercises were invaluable and indelible.

Sell the customer, only then the product. Spend time having that customer become comfortable with you. Build trust. Express interest in the life of the person you hope to persuade. Proceed to formal business only when the person to whom you are relating seems ready.

Practice. Learn from each encounter. What might you have said differently to interest and engage the other party on the telephone? Try again.

Decades later it became clear that I had internalized these guidelines. I found myself using the same approach, the identical sales devices, to raise funds from donors, to recruit new trustees, and to develop a relationship with journalists.

That seven-year-old pridefully observed his father, the mutual fund salesman par excellence. He emulated him. The impact has lasted a lifetime.

Once learned well, sales is the epitome of the transferable skill. Whether you find that some variation of sales is how you'd like to spend your entire professional life, or whether you move on to another line of work, the capability you will have acquired is invaluable.

From the vantage point of sales or another important area of pursuit, the time may come when on-the-job training has reached its limit. You could well be ready for more formal educational opportunities.

If and when pursuing an advanced degree in, say, business, law, design, or accounting seems most sensible, then your employer may well be prepared to pay for all or much of tuition and room and board. In addition, nowadays, professional schools have developed excellent continuing education certificate programs that run from three to six intense weeks, or during the summer, or over many consecutive weekends. These total immersion experiences allow you to network with peers as well as to acquire job-related skills. Even more frequently than with formal degree programs, employers fully subsidize such offerings for high-potential staff.

Employees can rise in a firm without the benefit of postcollege formal education. Much depends on the employer's size, sophistication, and expectations of you. And for those who wonder whether there is a way to engage in the intellectual exploration that my postgraduate degree programs afforded me without pursuing them formally, my answer is yes. You can come very close through a combination of rigorous reading, observing classes as an unmatriculated guest, and finding like-minded peers with common interests.

Even in the face of my cautions and reservations, illustratively, if you are ready to pursue an MBA or a law degree, the experience can be powerful, both intellectually and for your career prospects.

Knowing your way around a balance sheet and an operating statement. Learning how to design products and services, how to source and price them, and how to market and sell them to compete successfully. Studying styles of leadership and understanding the importance of organizational culture. These are just a few of the many skills, insights, and bits of knowledge that you will take away from the MBA classroom and deliver to the workplace.

As in business school, mastering fact patterns in hundreds of cases is a vital discipline in the law. Weighing evidence and applying rules to the issues at play. Mastering the art of posing that penetrating question to colleagues, witnesses, juries, and judges. Switching roles and moving from protagonist to antagonist, from counsel for the defense to prosecutor. Learning the rules of torts, contracts, civil procedure, criminal law, among other subjects, and how they have evolved. These are mere glimpses at what law school has in store for you.

Immersing yourself in business or legal education in the company of professors who know what they are about and of highly motivated students can be thrilling. You come away not just with analytical, rhetorical, and writing skills and with substantive knowledge, but also with the self-confidence needed to master new situations and to rise to sudden, often unexpected challenges at work.

What's more, many of those you encounter at graduate school can become lifelong allies as you confront knotty workplace difficulties and as you progress on an exciting career path.

## Sign Me Up

As you approach retirement age, it is not too late to reinvent yourself.

I have counseled many women and men in the third or fourth quarter of their careers to consider activities that will take fullest advantage of a life filled with productive work and valuable experience.

Whether through teaching, tutoring, coaching, or mentoring, engagement with the younger generation can bring with it enormous satisfaction. Helping a child to read or compete or become a better athlete is an enduring gift. Transferring the skills of a mechanic, plumber, or woodworker to an initiate is a critical investment. So is teaching the fine points of management and leadership.

These tutorial experiences can take place in a workshop, on the factory floor, on a playing field, or in an office. They can occur in a formal setting like a lecture hall or classroom, in a one-on-one instructional session at a community center, or at home. And they can be accomplished in a for-profit, nonprofit, or governmental environment.

What matters most is the match between an individual or organizational need and the earned pleasure of helping to satisfy it.

Service on nonprofit boards of directors, in community advisory groups, or in Boys or Girls Clubs can also bring much satisfaction. When Peggy Noonan wrote the phrase "A thousand points of light" for President George H. W. Bush, she had in mind volunteering in any of the multitude of institutions that comprise America's Third Sector.

Of course, participation in the electoral process, in government service, may also be part of an "it's never too late" strategy.

It helps a great deal if during your active professional career time was set aside for meaningful involvement with nonprofits, in the electoral process, or in other dimensions of public life. Those who have devoted many years to these realms of activity are prideful of the expertise and experience needed to perform well in them. Such practitioners are understandably wary of inexperienced latecomers who, because they were successful in the private sector, believe that civil service is relatively easy and straightforward.

The former head of Merrill Lynch, Don Regan, who served as President Reagan's chief of staff for a brief, stormy, and unproductive period, or Rex Tillerson, former CEO of Exxon Mobil, who may rank as the worst-performing secretary of state in American history, belie such a naive expectation.

Gaining some familiarity with key figures and issues before trying on a new role for size is advisable. Even the best of tailors insists on several fittings before a custom-made suit is ready for wearing.

# The Search for Meaningful Work Starts Early and May Never End

1. The earliest years of life, from birth to six, are as or more important than any other period in shaping emotional, behavioral, and cognitive development. Parents and other caregivers should act accordingly.

2. Achieving a work-life balance is virtually impossible at any given time. But the demands of the workplace and a private life can be satisfied *over time*. Strong partners at home, a supportive workplace, and a network of friends and family are indispensable to finding a sense of equilibrium between life at home and the realities of employment.

3. As a general rule, schools educate. Employers train. That's the division of labor in America. Some change is in the air and on the way, like the growth of vocational and apprenticeship opportunities. Such a trend is highly unlikely to rapidly transform the basic pattern of who does what in the classroom and in the marketplace.

4. The college years can be critical in preparing yourself to learn, to communicate well orally and in writing, to solving problems as part of a team or independently, to listening carefully... Use them well. They can prepare you for a lifetime of continuing education and improvement.

5. Beyond fostering knowledge and capability, schools can be a vital source of connection to workplace opportunity. Your fellow students, faculty, and, most importantly, the alumni body can help identify desirable positions and vacancies throughout your career.

6. When choosing between workplace experience and graduate school, except in unusual circumstances, opt for the

former. There is no substitute for real jobs and occupational challenges. The sooner you experience them, the
better. Few are ever hurt by deferring advanced education
for several years or more after graduating from college. To
the contrary.

7. As you think about relevant jobs, consider the sprawling
   nonprofit sector and the sales function in any field of interest as potential entry-level jobs. There are millions of
   them. What you learn is portable. The skills you acquire
   are transferrable. They can last a lifetime.

8. Take full advantage of the longevity that advances in
   medicine and public health have helped to achieve. The
   gift of a longer life allows all of us more opportunity to
   change careers, or to volunteer our services to individuals
   or organizations, or to become involved in public service.
   The sixties and seventies may be perfect decades to recon-
   figure your professional trajectory, once again.

# – 4 –

# Persuading the Target Employer

---

One of the most formidable challenges to securing an appeal-ing job is gaining the attention of the prospective employer. How do you reach the hiring authority with clear, compelling, and persuasive messages? How do you break through the clutter of very busy lives to leave a favorable impression? How do you proceed with sensitivity and tact while remaining persistent and focused?

Communication to a prospective employer works best when it assumes the form that the recipient finds most convenient and comfortable. Your preferences do not count. What matters is the situational setting and the operating style of whomever you wish to reach. Your laser-like focus must be on pleasing the decision maker.

Doing so can be accomplished by email, by letter, by telephone, or by face-to-face meeting. These options are enumerated in reverse order of preference. The closer you are able to be physically to the hiring authority, the better your chances for success. Landing that telephone appointment or meeting often takes some time. It gener-ally needs to be preceded by written messages.

Ideally, you can identify a friend, peer, colleague, customer, cli-ent, or close associate of the prospective employer. Be sure that this source of connection is well-known to, and highly regarded by, the hiring authority. A passing acquaintance, or an offhand relationship, is not good enough. When you are confident about the strength of that bond, ask the contact to call or write touting you and the desirability of your being considered for the relevant job opening. After one or more of such introductory calls, the way is clear for you to follow up, referencing the mutual associate(s) and explaining the source of your interest in the vacancy. You should also express the desire to learn more about the opportunity and why you can seize it, if an offer eventually comes your way.

You must deliver a persuasive message. You need to explain why your experience, skills, knowledge, and/or potential uncannily match an institution's needs. The case you advance cannot be generic or boilerplate. It must be specific, tailored to the realities of a particular business, nonprofit, or government agency. And it must be concise.

A variation on the advice often given to public speakers applies as well to your formal written follow-up, after being favorably introduced. "Be brief. Be sincere. Be seated." To which I'd add, "Be quick."

The working days of busy people are crowded. It is critical to arrest the attention of a senior executive soon after the initial contact from a known and trusted source. Otherwise, the trail will run cold. Curiosity about you will dissipate. The standard operating search routines will then take over.

In any institutional process, including hiring, a leading question should always be on your mind: What's next?

In other words, how do you proceed after your initial written communication is received? Your letter or email, for example, might suggest that you will be calling for an appointment at the office. Then send a copy of your note to whoever helped you with an introduction, conveying your thanks and providing an alert to your proposed next step.

Do not neglect the personal assistant to the executive you are attempting to reach. Whoever occupies that position is very often the trusted guardian at the gate, heavily influencing, if not controlling, access to the boss. Learn his or her name. Try to engage in conversation. Be polite. *Please* and *thank you* are magic words. Use them. There is a tendency to label intermediaries or direct reports to the boss you are trying to corral as obstacles to access and to treat them brusquely or routinely.

Instead, befriend them. Regard executive secretaries, administrative aides, and human resource professionals as potential allies. They can open doors for you. They can secure time with the decision maker you need to reach. They may even be asked by the boss for an opinion about your style and demeanor. Do not ignore, let alone ride roughshod over them.

Keeping in touch with the network of supporters whom you gather and grow is indispensable to career advancement. Those who assist you need to feel highly valued. Inform them of your progress or of your setbacks in a timely fashion. That kind of positive reinforcement is more than polite. It is motivational. Hearing from you will encourage a pre-existing fan to keep you in mind for current and future opportunities. If your allies are the subject of benign neglect, if they feel taken for granted, then you run the risk of losing valuable supporters.

It is a judgment call as to whether you should attach a résumé to your initial email or letter. If you can incorporate its key elements into your brief letter, then by all means do so. Statements about your relevant past experience and who else knows you well are most important. As you attempt to be seriously considered as a candidate, impose as little as you can on the reader. Enclosing documents, or writing at length, is likely to do more harm than good.

For this very reason, sending out résumés cold or placing cold calls to prospective employers rarely works. Very few cull through unsolicited appeals as a way to triage applicants. That process is just too time-consuming. Few employers trouble to dive into a résumé haystack in the hope of finding that needle! Even fewer return the phone calls of those they do not know who are seeking work. These are examples of why the Lord created human resources departments. And even they are often unresponsive to veritable strangers.

Instead, spend your precious time deciding which openings really appeal to you and for which you are most qualified. Then think comprehensively and creatively about who knows whom at the target employer and how best to ask supporters for specific, focused help. Render it as easy as possible for a trusted intermediary to come to your assistance by specifying who needs to be reached, in what form, when, and with what message. If your contact is inclined to help you, explicit direction will not cause offense. It will be welcomed.

And if you ever need to use a résumé, reduce its content to the essentials. Craft the written distillation of your experience to fit the job to which you are applying. One-size-fits-all generic statements will not work. Eliminate unnecessary details like the high school you attended, your voluntary activities, certificates attesting to your having audited executive education programs, and the like. But do pay careful attention to form. The size of the font and the typeface. The design of the page. The ease with which what you send can be read. These features of the résumé can catch the eye and rivet attention.

Some job counselors encourage elaborating on a list of the positions you have held by summarizing the results you achieved at each step in your career. I have never been a fan of the adage that nothing succeeds like excess. Your rendition of results achieved is best left to a later stage in the employment exercise. Its coverage in a résumé is more likely to turn off a reader intolerant of surplus verbiage. Although intended to entice a prospective employer, avoid prolixity. There will be time to elaborate further on in the hiring process. Conveying such information early in the mating dance is simply too much, too soon. Don't risk burying the lede in first approaching the potential employer.

Another step well worth taking is to scrub your own digital trail—like postings on social media such as Facebook, Twitter, and Instagram that might leave a bad impression or be a potential source of embarrassment. You should also perform a Google search on yourself. It is very helpful for you to become fully acquainted with what a potential employer can readily learn from publicly available sources.

Following a phone call or meeting, a quick response is important. A timely note registers. It should crystallize the conversation, express warm thanks for it, and highlight your continued, ardent interest in the opportunity. If you are uncertain as to whether an email or an old-fashioned letter would be more appreciated, communicate both ways: by email, with hard copy to follow.

It is so easy for your correspondent to fail to notice your email in the avalanche of other messages contained in a busy executive's electronic in-box. Even if the faster communication is noticed, the snail mail follow-on becomes a useful reminder. Rarely, if ever, does its receipt arouse objection.

Paying close attention to the content and style of what you put on paper or transmit electronically will help to leave a favorable impression. Writing is a powerful tool. It can encapsulate the homework you have done on the firm and the care with which you listened to your interviewer. It can be a potent source of appeal and persuasion.

Too often, candidates treat such written forms of communication nonchalantly. These are not minor, inconsequential messages. Take them seriously. Avoid going through the motions. Someone on the other end may just care a lot about the content of your statement. Remember, whatever you send is likely to be circulated to all concerned parties in the firm. It may become the subject of careful review and discussion. Proceed accordingly. Consider asking a close friend to review your written submission for clarity and even to detect grammatical errors.

Often, standing between you and your would-be employer is the search firm retained by the hiring executive or a committee. Nowadays, the quest for a CEO, COO, or CFO rarely occurs without the multifaceted research, candidate sourcing and interviews, reference checks, and evaluation memoranda provided by a professional recruiting enterprise. Generally the search is carried out by women and men who can make their way through big data analytics and who know their way around a boardroom.

## The Search Firm: Assets and Cautions

If your experience is like mine, your first contact with a search firm will be on a cold call. Some staff member on an assignment from a Spencer Stuart or a Russell Reynolds or a Heidrick & Struggles will introduce herself and ask for information.

It could be an open-ended inquiry, requesting that you identify a colleague who might compete to fill a vacant post. It might be about someone who supplied your name as a reference for a job. During the course of the conversation, questions may also be asked about you. Not infrequently, the call to identify other names may also be a veiled way of testing your own availability and interest in a particular opening or in a future move.

With the connection established, an email job description is usually sent to you as a follow-up and a reminder. By passing along an excellent name or two to the firm, you are established as a cooperative, well-connected party.

Besides the three search firms mentioned above, Isaacson Miller, Phillips Oppenheim, and Korn Ferry are among those with which I have dealt most often. They all develop information on potential candidates for existing job searches or future openings. Having your name in their databases can be very useful.

Think of ways to encourage professionals at search firms to become your environmental scans. Their senior recruiters can call attention to openings of which you may be unaware and for which you may be highly qualified. If you are ready for a move and your interest is piqued, the search firm may then include your name on a preliminary list of candidates that is transmitted to the client for initial review.

Most journalists treat their reliable sources favorably. When provided with useful information, even if on deep background and not for attribution, they are more likely to favorably mention you in other articles or give you the benefit of the doubt if you become the subject of a reported piece. The executive recruiter is no different. If you have been forthcoming and cooperative when called about other searches, leaving a favorable impression in your wake, then when a relevant job opening emerges, thoughts may well turn in your direction.

Over time your contacts at these firms may become fairly regular. When you are a trusted, helpful figure, reciprocity rules. The firm begins to welcome your unsolicited suggestions about friends, colleagues, or mentees who are in, or on the threshold of crossing into, the job market. Your request for an informational, getting-to-know-one-another meeting for your referral will often be honored.

In any case, the recruiter is likely to keep you in mind when germane job openings surface. Then a member of the search team will interview you as part of a preliminary screening process. The results will be distilled in writing. Profiles like your own will be forwarded to search committee members or some other screening mechanism, the better to reach informed decisions about who is worthy of a formal interview.

It is important that you attempt to impress the search firm representative during these interactions. While senior recruiters rarely determine who wins the competition for any particular post, these professionals are important gatekeepers. If they judge you to be attractive, compelling, and versatile, it is likely that they will surface other job openings should you not succeed in the one for which you are currently being considered.

Help the professionals to help you. Since someone on the search team will be writing a description of you as a job candidate, keep that process as easy as possible. Supply up-to-date information about yourself, crafted with the particular job opening in mind. The beleaguered recruiter assigned to prepare these write-ups will be eager to utilize what you supply by way of background and qualification. If it can be used as received without much change, gratitude will come your way.

Likewise, critical information that can assist you in preparing for an interview will be compiled by the firm if you ask. Focus on requesting data and perspectives not readily available from public sources. Organizational charts. Recent internal or external executive speeches. Meeting minutes. Biographical profiles of senior staff and of directors or trustees. Such items can provide you with an insider's vantage.

It is important to keep in mind that as friendly and helpful as the recruiter may appear to be, it is the hiring employer who is the client. That can mean you may be asked to show up for a first or second interview, even though the firm knows that you do not rank high on the list of desirable candidates. Or you may be told that you are *the* finalist, when, in fact, you are being courted only in the event that the real preferred candidate declines the job offer late in the search or is surprisingly and unexpectedly not tendered a formal offer.

Having myself been the recruiter's bridesmaid but not the bride, I know how uncomfortable playing that role can be. You can feel used, even abused. Your time may seem to have been wasted. You have even run the risk of your current employer learning about your wanderlust. Still, such investments of energy may pay handsome dividends in the future. Moving through search processes is very useful practice. Postmortems about how you might have presented yourself more convincingly in writing or in person will inform your next opportunity. Competing for desirable posts is draining. There is nothing like losing to concentrate the mind. Defeat should lead to improvement. But only if you are willing to view setbacks as invaluable occasions to learn and grow.

Search firms do attempt (or pretend) to develop a relationship with you. As a practical matter, their business model is highly transactional. No recruiter is paid for prolonged or elongated searches. Profit margins depend on the efficiency and effectiveness of each search. A key measure is the number of clients per year per recruiter. Another metric is the annual revenue each recruiter generates from his or her book of business.

If quality-control benchmarks are not introduced at every stage of the firm's work, from inception to conclusion, speed can result in sloppiness, and efficiency can just mean that candidate write-ups, sourcing, and reference checking become routine, even mediocre, exercises.

Ultimately, the victims of any slipshod conduct are the clients. The revolving door of searched-for CEOs at the Museum of Art and Design, the International Museum of Contemporary Art in Los Angeles, El Museo del Barrio, and Lincoln Center are illustrations of such search-firm deficiencies. So was the undetected falsification of records very belatedly discovered in the president of the American Academy of Arts and Sciences and in the recent appointment, followed by a quick resignation, of the president of Hobart and William Smith Colleges.

The assignment of culpability is best demonstrated by the guarantee offered by all firms. If the accepted candidate is fired for cause or resigns within one year of hire, the firm will conduct a second search free of charge. That guarantee is a virtual admission of responsibility. It is an attempt to be held accountable for errors of omission or commission.

Why a self-respecting enterprise would return to the very firm that recommended a failed candidate mystifies me. In fact, many clients absorb the loss of fees expended and time invested and simply move on. And because the first search firm's performance is not often publicly disclosed, real accountability rarely occurs. Lackluster service or deficient judgment is treated with impunity. The poorly handled client just swallows hard and returns to the marketplace for leadership talent.

Whatever the strengths or weaknesses of search-firm performance, your candidacy is largely in your own control. Seek the best information and perspective you can acquire from the search firm of record, but do not be overly dependent on it. Be helpful to recruiters and cooperate with them. They often learn of opportunities early. They can clue you in to job openings. They can offer you helpful advice during the entire exercise.

Search processes are quirky. The hiring employers can be fickle. Candidates are not always treated fairly.

All of this aside, you are largely the master of your own fate. Who you are and how you comport yourself ultimately rule the day.

No matter what stage of executive development you may be pursuing, little is more important than your face-to-face encounters with the hiring employer. You may be entering the job market for the first time or hoping to change positions within your current firm. You could be compelled to look for work by an involuntary layoff or by volition, seeking to leave your current workplace in search of the new and the different. Perhaps you are reinventing yourself for a final lap or two of business life. Regardless of the circumstances or the motivation, performing well when interviewed is indispensable to being hired.

# − 5 −

# The Interview

_____

The résumé you transmitted to that desirable employer and the follow-up phone conversation seem to have worked. Contacts from your friends, colleagues, or acquaintances intended to secure you a spot on the interview schedule probably helped as well.

Or, perhaps, that gatekeeper search firm has included you in a preferred circle of candidates.

Whatever the cause, you have already overcome a few formidable obstacles on the way to an attractive job offer.

Now comes the formal interview.

Careful, thorough, and thoughtful preparation for this encounter will serve you well.

Begin by learning all you can about those with whom you will be speaking. What are their formative educational and professional experiences? How did each member of the interview team become associated with the organization you wish to join? What continues to attract them to it?

Appealing to the interests and ideals of search committee members or hiring executives is easier when you have learned a lot about them. If you can naturally weave into your responses to questions reference to the personal, professional, and civic lives of interviewers, so much the better. Nowadays, a simple Google search and a hard look at a Wikipedia profile will probably provide ample clues and cues to facilitate conversation.

Of course, you will also need to learn all you can about the organization you hope to join. Prominent features of its history. The lively challenges and opportunities that are in its future. The track record of key players who might become your colleagues. As you study operating statements, balance sheets, annual reports, senior executive speeches, media coverage, and regulatory filings, start to compose the narrative that will define your candidacy.

Be prepared to explain why you really want this job and what leaves you confident that you could perform in it with distinction. Avoid platitudes and glittering generalities as you respond to questions. But also refrain from being cocky and displaying a know-it-all confidence. Both styles are off-putting.

Instead, identify general directions for the institution, areas of activity that must be tackled or can be improved. Highlight these even as you stress the need to spend the first few weeks and months listening carefully to a substantial cross-section of employees, clients, investors, and other stakeholders, in order to learn of their concerns, priorities, and aspirations.

Remember, the organization you are commenting on is the pride and joy of some, if not all, of the search committee members with whom you are speaking. What you critique may have been their creation or, at the very least, may have enjoyed their approval. On the other hand, trustees have a right to expect that they are conversing with more than an empty suit or a potted plant. They should feel that you have studied the job you covet and developed some tangible thoughts about its future.

Ideally, what begins as a Q&A session becomes a lively conversation. If you are uncertain of the meaning of a remark, request clarification or elaboration. Don't hesitate to ask for reactions to your ideas or whether your initial responses to questions are on the mark. The very best encounters should leave search committee members charmed and disarmed, wondering who really interviewed whom!

The content of what you say matters, of course. But so does how you carry yourself during the course of the meeting. Poise, self-confidence, lucidity, and a sense of comfort are all highly valued. So is a sense of humor. Take command of the room by virtue of your posture, eye contact, nonverbal communication skills, and firm handshake.[1]

Remember, your answer to any question is less important than the overall impression you leave. And that composite view of you is likely to be formed very early in the meeting. Once set, it is often difficult to change during the course of an interview.

So, listen to what your mother probably taught you and act accordingly. Arrive early. Pay attention to what you wear and how well you are groomed. Summon positive energy for the occasion. And smile whenever appropriate.

Exhibiting a sense of composure reflects your inner security and comfort. Try to relax.

Self-assured enthusiasm is a highly desirable and communicable trait. Those who conduct the interview are drawn to all who embody it.

If there is a search firm involved, the lead professional can offer useful guidance on what to expect. Who will attend. The biographies of the participants. The key issues on their minds. How many other candidates are in contention. How long the session is expected to last.

Take full advantage of this resource. After all, the search firm is well served by delivering thoroughly prepared, vetted, and impressive candidates to its client. And your continued connection to a Korn Ferry, Heidrick & Struggles, or Spencer Stuart is important to maintain, whether or not you win any particular competition.

By performing well and remaining upbeat at the interview, you will stay high on the candidate list of one or more such firms.

One tricky challenge worth pondering is how to present yourself favorably while avoiding boasts and self-inflation. When asked a question that calls for self-assessment, I have always responded with modesty and then referred to others who are in a better position to appraise my on-the-job performance. For example, those who reported to me and those at whose pleasure I served. Colleagues. Trustees. Peers. Investors. Donors. Journalists.

Because it is likely to prove useful, I bring with me a list of references that details names, institutional affiliations, and profession. In assembling it, I, of course, focus on those who think of me favorably and, importantly, whom I have reason to believe members of the search committee may know. For convenience, the current email address and phone numbers of all are provided, and each member of the search committee is handed a copy.

It never fails—attention is quickly drawn to familiar names.

"How do you know her?"

"I wasn't aware that he was so interested in that organization you helped lead. What caused the connection?"

"Do you have any objection to any of us calling people on that list?"

The answer to that last question is simple and clear.

"No, not at all. Please feel free to reach out to any of those twenty names. Of course, only a few of them are aware of my involvement in this search, so the purpose of your call will be a surprise. But I feel no need to alert any of them in advance. Everyone listed knows me well."

It never fails—soon after the interview, several search committee members will contact their clients, friends, colleagues, or associates. The objective of this exercise from the applicant's point of view is to have others, third parties, evaluate favorably your performance and advance your candidacy, rather than engaging in self-praise. And the fringe benefit is that some of those called may let you know what's on the mind of key search committee members who reached out to them.

That is valuable information. It helps you, the candidate, prepare for a second interview, if the search committee decides another is needed.

In sum, there are two reasons why that distributed list of references can be so useful.

First, you have rendered it easy for search committee members to follow up with handpicked references. Digging deep into your past and inquiring after former colleagues and associates whom you do not identify is hard, painstaking, time-consuming work. That is precisely why it so rarely happens. Left to their own devices, reference checks of search firms are often spotty, inconsistently applied to competing candidates, and poorly executed. Penetrating questions that reveal matters of character, emotional IQ, treatment of peers and subordinates, and sheer work ethic are often not asked.

This lapse frequently explains search failures and selections that just do not work.

Second, search committee members and employers are often overly influenced by the judgment of social and professional peers, even when the candidate's experience on which they are commenting is largely unrelated to the job at hand. Former national security adviser and secretary of state Condoleezza Rice and former secretary of defense Robert Gates were the most forceful proponents of Rex Tillerson to be appointed and then confirmed by the United States Senate as President Trump's first secretary of state. Their support turned out to be insufficiently grounded in relevant experience with him—embarrassingly so. Having significantly weakened the Foreign Service, having neglected to pay attention to the very State Department he was selected to lead, having failed to cultivate members of the press or key figures in Congress, Secretary Tillerson was off to a very disappointing start. This neglect was compounded by the expressed loss of confidence in him from the president. As a result, Tillerson's year-long tenure was stormy and inconsequential and called into question the judgment of Rice and Gates.[2]

At the time, however, their voices were deemed powerful and persuasive.

Beware. This is often the case with impressive VIPs providing references. They need to be cross-examined in order to determine how well they *really* know the candidate. Have they given sufficient thought to the relevance of their prior experience with that individual to the specific challenge at hand? In approaching influential, notable personalities to support your candidacy for a job, be certain they understand the essence of the position and the major reasons why you are perfectly fit for it.

Three important lessons emerge from these examples.

First, it hardly hurts to identify well-known names who can favorably comment on your past performance and potential.

Second, when selecting references whom you wish to be called so that they can speak on your behalf, endeavor to coach any who need it on the connection between their knowledge of you and the new job you hope to secure.

Finally, when you are being interviewed for a job, the assessment undertaken is in part personal. Does your potential employer like you? Can you be trusted? Will colleagues enjoy being around you? In responding to questions, please try to remember how much your potential employer wishes to feel comfortable in your presence and in working at your side.

I was reminded of this issue of likability when competing for the post as president of Lincoln Center. Apparently, the first interview had gone well. The search committee members came away persuaded that I understood the complex dynamics of Lincoln Center and the clear and present challenges confronting it. Most were convinced that I could take the lead in overcoming the formidable economic, diplomatic, and managerial obstacles immediately ahead.

Indiscreetly, one of the favorably impressed members called a mutual friend requesting that he convey a message to me. It was simple—loosen up. Apparently, I had come across as very knowledgeable and well prepared, but much too serious, antiseptic, even cold. The advice was blunt: tell your friend to let his sense of humor and ability to work with others shine through during his next search committee encounter.

It was the fall and winter of 2001, and the recently concluded presidential race between Al Gore and George Bush was still fresh on the minds of the politically conscious. It occurred to me, suddenly, that from a personality perspective, the members of the search committee would prefer having a beer with Bush. I was coming off too much like Gore, too distant, even severe.

So advised, in my next interview, I told a few jokes, some of them self-deprecating, a few actually funny. For example, when I was asked about any unique qualities or experience that I could bring to the job, I recall saying, "Well, from the contentious Lincoln Center environment you have been describing, perhaps the campus could use UN peacekeeping troops. As the president of the International Rescue Committee, I am in a good position to have them summoned to the Upper West Side." I volunteered some flattering knowledge about several key search committee members who didn't mind being praised in front of their peers, and I stressed how much I enjoyed working with trustees and volunteers to achieve important objectives.

As Maya Angelou memorably put the matter: "People will forget what you said. People will forget what you did. But people will never forget how you made them feel."

And part of what your employer feels is related to the immediacy, the warmth, and the authenticity of your thank-you. Email your genuine expression of appreciation soon after the interview is completed, if the process is on a fast track. Consider a handwritten note if the search proceedings are moving at a more relaxed pace. Craft your message to be as true to the actual experience as possible. Never fail to reiterate your enthusiasm for the job and your desire to be selected.

Please remember to request in advance that time be left for you to ask interviewers about matters on your mind. Ideally, the way you ask and answer questions will lead to a conversation that everyone enjoys.

Also, be absolutely certain to formulate some key messages you wish to leave with those interviewing you. The dominant impression left by this occasion should be under your control. Do not let it slip away. Never forget to stress how much you'd like to be hired, why, and what kind of positive impact your leadership can leave on the organization, its employees, and the clients it serves.

All of these tips may appear easy to remember. Yet, candidates lose their composure. Nervousness creeps into their voice and manner. Time slips away. Interviewees fail to be concise. They ramble on to no particular advantage. They do not establish eye contact with their interviewers. They do not take into account the nonverbal reactions to their comments and fail to react to them. They appear awkward and uncomfortable, rather than loose, focused, and energetic.

Such a demeanor takes over too often. Anxiety rules. Clear thinking and spot-on reactions become the exception rather than the rule.

The causes of this breakdown are many and varied. Not studying the organization enough in advance. Not becoming familiar with your interlocutors and their backgrounds. Not being sufficiently conscious of the need to persuade others of the relevance of your experience, abilities, and skills to the current vacancy. Not rehearsing for the encounter.

Instead, imagine the questions that might be asked, think about the background of those who will put them to you, and test the persuasiveness of your answers with friends and colleagues who are veterans of such interviews.

Newcomers to the interview experience are naturally prone to less-than-optimal comportment. But I have also noticed that poor performers at interviews are often CEOs and senior executives who have held the job they currently occupy for relatively long periods of time.

As a result, they too are unaccustomed to the competitive job marketplace. They are unfamiliar with the need to sell themselves. They believe that what they have accomplished should be compelling enough on its merits. They take modesty, humility, and self-effacement to extremes. They often exhibit hesitancy and discomfort. They are rusty.

It is not by accident that interviews are major challenges to candidates aspiring to be selected for a desirable post.

The equivalent in politics are debates, for presidential, congressional, and state and local competitions for office.

The equivalent in federally appointed positions is testifying in front of the US Senate in confirmation hearings, as part of the constitutional advise and consent process.

The equivalent in sports is tennis.

The intensity of preparation by the protagonist is critical.

There is no one but you who calls the plays or plans strategy at halftime, as in football or basketball.

There is no one to call time-outs, to slow down a game and offer tactical support, not to mention a coach's cheerleading, as in basketball.

No huddles or time-outs are permitted.

In tennis, as in debates, as in confirmation hearings, you are on your own. All training, practice, and strategy need comprehensive attention well before the anticipated matchup.

And so it is with job interviews. A good place to begin is by reviewing these sample questions and devising answers you find persuasive.

## Ten Likely Interview Questions

1. Your experience seems somewhat at odds with the post you are seeking (candidate now lives and works in another city, labors in another field of interest, operates in a much larger or smaller organization). Why isn't the adjustment to this very different assignment too risky, a bridge too far?

2. It is often observed that there is more to be learned from failure than from success. Identify a recent mistake of your own and what you learned from this error of judgment.

3. Management is a process of continuous improvement. What aspect of your operating style needs remedial work?

4. You have read about our organization and spoken to people familiar with it. We appreciate that there is much more for you to learn. Nonetheless, in broad strokes, tell

us what you now see as the most important objectives to be accomplished during your tenure. As you now understand the organization, what would be your priorities in year one on the job?

5. What is it about this position that you find most attractive?

6. What is it about this position that concerns you the most?

7. Is there anything we should know about your physical health, emotional well-being, or family situation that might influence the efficiency, effectiveness, or creativity of your performance at work?

8. What do you most enjoy doing when you are not at work?

9. For what length of time, how many years, do you envision yourself serving in this post?

10. Name several of the books, films, plays, or performing arts events that most influenced or impressed you over the last year. What about them is memorable?

## The Employer Perspective

These challenging questions raise another: how your potential employer views the hiring process. For both parties, the job seeker and the talent scout, a key to success is empathy. Understanding the motivations and points of view of your opposite number eases the way to filling that highly desirable job opening or recruiting that much-sought-after talent.

As a job candidate, it is good to spend time figuring out what may be on the employer's mind. What needs, issues, and concerns are most salient for the recruiter? How will the candidate screening process influence the selection? Who are the real decision makers and what professional strengths do they most prize?

Having identified fully with the candidate, it is now time to switch sides. Let's delve into the factors that influence employer choice.

Understanding the employer's point of view will do more than help you win the competition to fill a desirable opening. Learning how an employer conducts its business will also assist you in determining whether you really wish to join the enterprise at all.

# The Competition for Talent

─────────────

*"Hire right, because the penalties for hiring wrong are huge."*
—Ray Dalio, *Principles*[1]

*"Why hiring is the single most important people activity in any organization."*
—Laszlo Bock, *Work Rules!*[2]

You cannot compete convincingly for desirable jobs without imagining how employers approach recruiting and without figuring out what they highly value. Conversely, employers cannot attract a generous share of talent without understanding what workplace attributes aspiring candidates cherish the most.

Neither party to the employment divide can just think about their own situation in isolation. Vying for talent means understanding the other side and empathizing with its desires and needs. The best way to keep terrific employees and captivate hot prospects is to consider their points of view. Concurrently, the best way to win that precious job is to think from the outside in. What is most desired by the employer I yearn to join? That question should remain fore-most in the mind of the aspirant.

While job candidates compete for desirable positions, employers are hard at work as well.

The best of them are in a constant, conscious struggle to figure out how to retain their most valuable employees and how to woo the most desirable newcomers to their ranks. They know that the scarcest resource in the combative marketplace is human talent.

> Bill Gates has said that if you took the twenty smartest people out of Microsoft it would be an insignificant company, and if you ask around the company what its core competency is, they don't say anything about software. They say it's hiring.[3]

Protagonists in this supply-and-demand equation perform much better when they understand the position of their opposite member.

Employees and aspiring candidates need to figure out what at-tributes employers hold in highest regard. How to leave them with a favorable impression, up to and including the interview, is a for-midable test of one's homework, network, sheer preparation, and interpersonal skills.

Successful employers and employees have at least two charac-teristics in common. They are always forward looking and market focused.

Just as it is far easier to retain a highly valued client than to obtain a new one, so the employer's aim to fill its ranks with highly motivated, gifted, driven staff begins with retaining high perform-ers now on payroll.

From the employer's perspective, in the competition for talent, the first imperative is to keep the valued contributors who are al-ready in its ranks. It is tempting to observe that the worst time to search for a superior employee is when you need one.

While it is true that the culture of an organization is set at the top, whether and how it is practiced day to day falls to line managers. Employees are most influenced by their immediate supervisor and their peers. If the CEO sets an example by precept and practice of caring about the welfare of colleagues, then word circulates quickly about how important are such values as dignity, respect, acknowledgment, recognition, and reward. A CEO who embodies the culture inevitably finds those values, beliefs, and conduct widely emulated.

Most organizations, whatever their formal modes of communication, also house a prison-quality grapevine. When a senior manager sends a personal note of appreciation or encouragement to an employee at work or at home, you can be sure that many others quickly learn of it. When spot bonuses are available to recognize superior performance, employees are motivated to earn them. When an employee's family member encounters a serious health crisis or other form of emergency and the organization rallies around with all kinds of material and moral support, the bond between the employee and the caring organization strengthens considerably.

Every employer would do well to focus creative energy on those identified as having high potential. Treating the professional development of each designee individually works wonders for morale, productivity, professional growth, and length of service.

- Would the high-potential employee benefit from specialized training and education within the organization, in professional associations, or at university offerings?

- Could the high-potential employee utilize the guidance of an assigned mentor?

- Is an apprentice relationship with a colleague of value?

- Might it be useful to arrange a series of one-on-one meetings with veterans inside and outside the organization carrying the dual purpose of finding out how others approach a business opportunity and broadening the network of a talented staffer?

- What do the future aspirations of the high-potential employee suggest for different job assignments, or for service on task forces commissioned by senior executives to figure out how to solve a problem or to seize an opportunity that crosses departmental boundaries?

- Are there specific skills—public speaking, analyzing financial statements, developing sales and marketing acumen—that a given high-potential employee would like to acquire?

Fashioning a custom-designed professional development program not only enriches the capability of high performers and extends their length of stay in the organization, but it also informs the process of succession planning. So does job sculpting.[4] Defined as the art of matching people to jobs by tailoring their future work assignments, or simply adding to an already existing set of responsibilities, or moving an employee to a new position, job sculpting seeks to guide people to duties they truly enjoy. Such a process results in purposeful and energetic employees occupying posts that appeal most to their skills, interests, and passions.

A sound management process also weighs which employees could be successor candidates for all key positions within the organization. With that goal in mind, these kinds of experiences, exposures, and training are highly desirable in order to prepare a prospect for promotion to a more senior role.

*As you consider whether to become a serious applicant, ask yourself whether many of these progressive, thoughtful personnel policies are embedded as standard operating practices of the target employer. Is the institution that has drawn your keen interest attuned to the needs and aspirations of its high-performing employees? Are such values as respect, continuous learning, investment in personnel, reward, and recognition part and parcel of the organization's culture?*

While these growth and development schemes and succession-planning disciplines seem self-evidently healthy, too often not much more than lip service is paid to them. Frequently, board members and trustees do not receive regular reports on the professional growth of high-potential executives. Often, succession planning is honored in the breach. Rather than human resource management being viewed as a strategic function fully worthy of CEO and director attention, it is consigned to a second-order priority.

Inevitably, a crisis reveals the high cost of neglect, and remedial action must be taken. Then a sudden sense of urgency arises.

Just as tone begins at the top, management stability and institutional solidarity do as well. So when a respected and well-liked chief executive or member of senior management announces a resignation, the risks to organizational continuity are high. Unless there is widespread dissatisfaction with the status quo and the staff responsible for it, the board of directors needs to be concerned about other defections of high-quality staff while a search for a successor is undertaken.

In this delicate vacuum, reassurance in the form of frequent communication to the senior team and to the employee body at large is critical. Also to be considered is the answer to this question: Who are the senior managers on which the future of the organization (and the success of the new CEO, when designated) will really depend? With the outgoing CEO's assistance, these vital few employees should be identified and retention bonuses offered to them.

By staggering the timing of these not insubstantial cash or stock awards, the new president or executive director can rely on a core team being in place to maintain momentum and to preserve institutional memory. Without such incentives, those facing the uncertainty of who a new leader will be and how they will fare as a result are more likely to look around. Sister organizations, rivals, and search firms, sensing a vulnerable period of transition, will be offering attractive options to the best and brightest.

Smart, shrewd organizations recognize these realities. They cannot be made to disappear. But steps like stay bonuses can help to mitigate them.

After all, it takes time to learn on the job. Forming an entirely new team is extremely difficult and requires several years. Sound management is almost always a blend of continuity and change.

The CEO's selection is a decisive inflection point for any organization. In politics, that process is called elections. In corporations and nonprofits, it is called search.

In examining search failures, the overwhelming cause can be reduced to six words: *poor process leads to poor outcomes*. That rule applies not only to finding the best available leader, but also to monitoring his or her performance.

One excellent and unorthodox way to really learn about the organization you may wish to join and whether to compete as an applicant is to peek behind its well-drawn curtains. Few outsiders ever learn what happens in grand jury proceedings, or behind the closed doors of a psychiatrist's office, or what any particular source discloses to a journalist. So it is with director or trustee deliberations in corporations or nonprofits.

By removing a veil of secrecy, I hope to inform you, the candidate, of what does, might, and should happen in the boardroom, generally. More particularly, how do directors and trustees conduct themselves when an opening in a CEO or other senior management post needs to be filled?

*Every job-finding exercise involves an attempt to find the answer to three fundamental questions. Is the position for which you are applying one that you would really like to fill? Is it lodged in an organization that will be challenging and fun, a place you would be proud to call your own? Can you be selected from among the many who are competing for that post?*

*You are engaged in a daunting process—trying to persuade the hiring authority that you are the perfect person to fill a vacancy, even as you are attempting to figure out whether the job is right for you.*

*Let's better understand the employer's point of view. Doing so is an excellent way to help you decide whether you want that job and, if so, how to win in the competition for it.*

Here is a checklist of key questions to keep foremost in mind when that critical post needs to be filled with the very best available candidate. Interspersed among the answers are lessons (like the two you have already seen). You, the candidate, can learn much from an employer's thought processes, practices, and procedures.

## 1. Who decides?

Either a search committee or an empowered senior executive should be designated to proffer recommendations to a higher authority, or to simply hire the preferred applicant without any required additional step.

Ideally, if there is a search committee, it should be comprised of trustees and/or senior executives, who represent a microcosm of the board or staff and who have won their trust and confidence. The committee members would best be selected by the board chair, by a duly constituted nominating and governance committee, or by a designated staff leader, taking into account tenure, gender, age, experience, ethnicity, perspective, and resources.

Among the questions to consider in forming the group are whether staff should be included, whether any non-board donors or emeriti belong, and what optimal size is both workable and broadly representative of institutional interests and constituencies.

The larger the group, the greater the likelihood that the strict confidentiality of the process will not be honored. Promising prospects, concerned about premature disclosure of their candidacy, or even the mere expression of interest in another institution, may well decline to participate. Besides, what was intended to be a heterogeneity of views can become an unmanageable babble of discordant voices. Recruiting can become contentious, time-consuming, and frustrating to the executive or the board of directors looking to hire needed personnel as soon as possible.[5]

Of course, the smaller the group, the more susceptible it is to accusations of elitism, with control lodging in a self-appointed, narrowly selected group of insiders.

How to balance these concerns and how to compensate for choosing the larger or smaller group is a critical leadership challenge.

If smaller, then even more communication and consultation with key stakeholders during the search process is the better part of wisdom. For example, asking finalist candidates to privately meet with some important players not serving on the search committee could prove very useful.

If larger, special care needs to be taken about the confidentiality of distributed written materials, the division of labor as to who speaks with whom and when, and limiting the number of meetings and the length of the process.

In either case, the search chair needs to ensure that no one or two members dominate the questions and the discussion that follows each interview. Personnel selection is an admixture of art, science, and human judgment. No one owns a monopoly on superior wisdom. Hopefully, a criterion for search committee member selection will be executives who have significant management and hiring experience. Trustees or outside directors who have been to this rodeo before are highly desirable.

Included in the search should be decision makers familiar with a lot of institutional history and with the process of personnel selection.

## 2. What search firm, if any, should be hired to assist and inform the process?

The selection of a search firm is important. How much experience has it enjoyed in the kind of challenge now before you? Do not hesitate to ask about specific cases. What did the firm learn from clients who credit it with success, and those who deem a given outcome to have failed? Who, precisely, will be in the lead on the search and why is the firm eager to take on this assignment? Is there anyone in the search firm who has successfully worked at a senior level for a comparable nonprofit or commercial enterprise?

If the firm under consideration is selected, how precisely will it recommend proceeding?[6]

Questions like these test the flexibility and resourcefulness of the firm. They also reveal whether you will look forward to spending several dozen hours with its principals. What's more, these interviews of competing search firms are a warm-up for search committee members who need to come to know one another and work as a team.

Ask about how the firm sources candidates, how it conducts preliminary interviews, and how many contenders it aims to bring to the attention of the hiring authority. Optimally, should the search committee be interviewing about six? More? Fewer? And from what larger pool of prospects will that number be drawn?

Do not hesitate to probe about related searches in the recent past that were the most disappointing for the firm and what it learned from the experience. Which recent searches did the firm compete to conduct and did not win? To what does it attribute those losses?

### 3. How will the selected firm be managed and in accordance with what specific guidelines?

As with any other supplier or contractor, how well the relationship with a search firm is managed determines whether you have extracted the maximum value from its work.

A lot can go wrong.

In sourcing, the firm can skim the surface of research databases instead of plumbing their depths. It can present candidates who have already been vetted or even interviewed in other searches, saving the firm precious time, but often serving up inappropriate, also-ran, "filler" applicants.

The narratives of candidate interviews can be shallow, ridden with clichés and bromides, or they can reveal difficult-to-acquire insights about the job seeker's past and promise.

In guiding the committee or the hiring executive, the firm can offer advice on the content and pacing of questions, on the style of participating members, on whether sufficient time is reserved for the candidate to express curiosities and concerns, and on the pros and cons of a second interview. Or the firm can function in relative silence, as if it were confined to auditing the content and handling the logistics of the day. How engaged the firm is will depend on what you ask of it and how open you are to advice when offered.

Reference checking can often be the Achilles' heel of a search firm's work. Interviewing only those names that a candidate provides is a sure sign of laziness. Brief and perfunctory interviews are another. If the firm fails to surface names to call who are familiar with the candidate's performance and character but are not volunteered by the job seeker, if the firm does not uncover any new observations from reaching to the candidate's direct reports or to colleagues at sister institutions or at professional associations, if the firm does not welcome sharing the reference checking task with search committee members, these may be telltale signs of trouble.

Kevin Ryan, the founder and CEO of DoubleClick, in an essay for the *Harvard Business Review*, argues that while companies always profess to believe employees are their most valuable asset, few of them act accordingly. He maintains that any hiring process has three dominant elements: the résumé, the interview, and the reference check. Of these, the reference check is by far the most important.

The résumé describes basic qualifications and not much else. Ryan has found a major problem with candidate interviews. It is virtually impossible to avoid being influenced by people who are well-spoken, self-confident, and physically attractive. Those characteristics are seductive and can lead you astray.

To learn about such important traits as whether the candidate listens well, pays attention to detail, works smoothly with others, and treats colleagues respectfully, you must look to references. And in doing so, it is imperative that you do not simply rely on the names that the candidate supplies.

Digging deep in such interactions uncovers much about emotional intelligence, about how the candidate manages under pressure, about whether he or she possesses a sense of humor and of history, widely distributes credit for success, and displays unimpeachable integrity. And because, according to Ryan, the CEO's most important job is attracting, retaining, motivating, and managing talent, he himself conducts many of these reference checks personally.[7]

To learn only after a failed search that the incumbent was drawn from a very small pool of candidates, or that preparatory interviews conducted by the search firm were perfunctory, or that reference checks were too small in number and too superficial in quality, is a recipe for keen disappointment. It is also entirely avoidable.

I know of few appointees judged to be on-the-job failures where the warning signs could not have been revealed in prior assignments or past personal behavior. The evidence often hides in plain sight. But uncovering the truth requires hard investigatory work. Without it, the risk is high that your search consultant is just going through the motions, cavalierly checking the boxes of a candidate's past conduct.

How else to explain the recent announcement that the president of Hobart College, my alma mater, abruptly resigned only nine months after his inauguration amid "sudden" findings of plagiarism?[8]

When no less prestigious a group than the American Academy of Arts and Sciences compels the resignation of its president, whom it found feigned having earned a PhD, what are we to conclude about the thoroughness of that search process? The president served as the CEO for over a decade. What are we to surmise about the due diligence of its board of directors?[9]

These are just two of many egregious cases of personnel malpractice that occur every year. Well beyond the rudimentary task of simply verifying credentials, there can also be shoddy and superficial background research. Shallow candidate pools. Deficient reference checks. Poorly written and incomplete interview summaries. These unacceptable inadequacies often do not take long to reveal themselves in a successful candidate's actual on-the-job performance.

Whether or not an outside consultant is retained, the frequent lack of thoroughness and discipline in hiring processes is horrifying. Such errors of commission and omission are readily found in the public sector and in commercial enterprises as well.

*How thoughtfully and competently has the hiring authority prepared itself to review and assess candidates? If you sense a lack of readiness for this crucial exercise, what might that explain about the merits of the employer, more generally?*

*Can you as a candidate actually benefit from the weaknesses readily apparent in the hiring process? Why not take it upon yourself to provide what ordinarily would be expected of the search firm, or the employer directly? Without being asked, supply many names of references, together with brief explanations of how they know you and easy-to-reach contact information. Compose a well-written biographical statement that is succinct, comprehensive, and user friendly. Help in other ways to prepare the search firm, or the lead recruiter, to brief the hiring committee about you.*

*Do not carp about the deficiencies you detect in the hiring process. Instead, turn them to your advantage.*

Just consider President Trump's appointments of Michael Flynn as his national security adviser or Matt Whitaker as acting attorney general, or Scott Pruitt as administrator of the Environmental Protection Agency, or Ryan Zinke as the secretary of the interior. President Trump even went so far as to suggest that his White House physician, Dr. Ronny Jackson, become the head of the Department of Veterans Affairs, the second-largest agency in the federal government and one for which Dr. Jackson had no management experience whatsoever. Within days of the announcement, Dr. Jackson withdrew his candidacy.

And even as I write, two announced candidates for the Federal Reserve Board, Herman Cain and Stephen Moore, were withdrawn from consideration before their formal submission to the United States Senate for review. Widely regarded as unqualified to serve, both Cain and Moore suffered as well from public revelations of personal embarrassments. As a result, more than a few *Republican* senators indicated that they could not vote for confirmation of either man. They and others publicly urged the president to vet candidates for key offices before disclosing their names publicly. In other words, the White House was being asked to enroll in a required course entitled Doing Your Homework 101.

Or consider the case of Elizabeth Holmes as the CEO of Theranos, or Marissa Mayer, the CEO of Yahoo, or Travis Kalanick as CEO of Uber, or Jeff Immelt as CEO of General Electric. Each in their own way could not perform capably as leaders of their respective firms and were dismissed belatedly or allowed to leave of their own accord and largely on their own timetable.

As is the case with any important supplier of services, a search firm needs to be very carefully selected and actively managed.

**4. Have you rigorously defined what the organization needs before you look for new talent?**

Even before a search-firm review process is undertaken, let alone when potential candidate names are tossed around, trustees or the senior executive team should define in writing the condition of the organization, its virtues, deficiencies, and blemishes. It should set forth with as much clarity as possible what the governing body aspires to accomplish in the years ahead.

Such a statement will serve as a point of departure for meaningful conversations with candidates. It will also help clarify the salient qualities of the leader who can, with the help of many others, realize those aspirations.

*Ideally, the written position statement of the hiring organization will be set in the context of its forward-looking priorities. If such objectives are not apparent and, if at least some of them are not specified during your interview, then you may be dealing with a confused, floundering employer.*

*Drawing that tentative conclusion may cause you to recoil. Who needs to enter such a state of disarray?*

*A starkly different reaction is also possible. You can welcome the absence of a well-developed plan for the future. That very void may leave plenty of room for you, if and when hired, to take the lead in formulating policy and building consensus.*

*How you react probably depends on your fidelity to the mission of the institution, to its history and its potential. Are they compelling enough to draw you into a planning vacuum? Are you willing to invest the time and energy required to help determine institutional direction and to resolve disputes about basic issues?*

An employer should ask itself, are we looking for a stabilizing or a disruptive force?

Do we need a leader with financial acumen and fundraising or sales prowess?

How important are external relationships, compared with internal challenges?

Are communication skills critical?

In the balance to be struck as between the IQ and EQ of the job seeker, which of these aptitudes is more important for success in the particular post being filled? How natively intelligent is the candidate? How sensitive to the personalities and points of view revealed by subordinates, peers, and higher authorities?

If there has been a president of a university who could serve with distinction as the CEO of the Mensa Society, surely Larry Summers would merit that high honor.

His resignation as the president of Harvard University, after only five years of tumultuous service, was, nonetheless, attributed to the absence of basic EQ skills: the ability to get along with others;

to listen attentively; to resist showing that he was the smartest in any room he occupied (from the classroom to the boardroom to the football stadium).

Organizations need change. Managerial pendulums swing. Opinions swirl. That is why thrashing out points of view on paper can be so important. Just sending the candidate mission boilerplate and annual reports elides vital questions.

## 5. Has a process been crafted to communicate search plans to all key parties and to solicit their views?

The search committee is a small subset of the board of directors or of the staff. Its members alone cannot set institutional priorities to inform the talent-finding process. The quest for new leadership is a perfect opportunity to survey the balance of trustees, the key staff (and via a tool like Survey Monkey, even the entire employee body), as well as important foundation, corporate, and government officials, elected or appointed.

All who care about the organization will welcome the chance to contribute their views about the kind of leader now needed. They will be flattered by the attention and will appreciate having their views taken into account. Many will register useful opinions to digest and consider.

Insularity is a danger to any organization. Being out of touch with those it serves, those it employs, and those who support it as donors or investors can be very dangerous. A wise committee chair will seize this opportunity to engage key institutional stakeholders. The search process is a terrific way to overcome any tendency toward self-imposed isolation.

## 6. Do the search committee members pledge adequate time to conduct their work?

The board chair must extract a commitment from all search committee members to treat this role as a priority. Otherwise, searches take longer than they should due to the unavailability of members.

It is difficult to imagine a more important assignment than serving on a search committee. Accordingly, the selection of its members should be scrupulous.

## 7. Are you clear about the cause(s) of the vacancy, and does its history provide any guidance in finding the right successor?

A common understanding about what animated the search forms a sound basis for deliberation.

Did the CEO, or a key member of the senior team, leave for a more attractive position elsewhere? Was the incumbent's tenure long enough to leave a body of accomplishment? Can the separation be characterized as friendly and voluntary, or as tension laden and compelled? Was parting company the result of a prior failed search process? If so, what went wrong?

Whatever animated the departure generates a set of realities that help to condition the search process as well as the environment in which the new executive will be expected to function.

In a healthy organization, a thorough exit interview to determine the reasons animating a departure should be standard operating procedure.

Often, patterns of neglect and abuse are uncovered that require remedial attention.

If such a process applies to a plain vanilla "ordinary" employee, how could it be avoided for the CEO or any other senior manager?

*Learn all you can about the whys and wherefores of the departure of the incumbent whom you hope to replace. At the appropriate time, ask to meet with that outgoing leader. If your candidacy is successful, it is quite likely that you will inherit the pattern of behavior that gave rise to the exit.*

*You are entitled to a search process characterized by frankness and transparency. If you suspect that is not the case, a healthy future for the CEO-trustee relationship may be very difficult to create, or to restore, or to sustain.*

### 8. How much time and effort are expended in sourcing candidates, customary and nontraditional, and how is labor divided between the client's ideas and those of the search firm?

When the client and the search firm view each other as partners, the prospects for success improve. The employer can recommend candidates to be researched and interviewed. It can suggest ideas for how candidates are to be found.

Search firms often gravitate to traditional employment sectors. Their experience and databases are siloed by field. The unorthodox idea that an excellent CEO of a museum of natural history might have served as a liberal arts college president,[10] or that the CEO of one of the nation's largest botanical gardens might come from a post as the development director of a library,[11] would not naturally occur to a typical search firm. These two examples are among the exceptions that prove the rule.

If the committee is interested in examining unorthodox candidates, it needs to demand to have them unearthed. Otherwise, the search firm will be tempted to take the path of least resistance, the course of action that demands the least time and work.

For example, university presidents typically come up from the ranks of academia. Well, tell that to New York University. It hired former congressman John Brademas. Purdue University recruited Mitch Daniels, the former governor of Indiana and a director of the Office of Management and Budget, to be its president. Texas A&M University selected Robert Gates, the former secretary of defense to Presidents Bush and Obama, to assume its CEO mantle.

Donna Shalala, the former secretary of health and human services under President Bill Clinton, also served as the president of the Universities of Wisconsin and Miami. Janet Napolitano, the former governor of Arizona and secretary of homeland security in the Obama administration, is now the president of the University of California.

By most accounts, these men and women have performed with distinction. They did not climb any kind of academic ladder or pedagogical pecking order.

Certainly, fame or novelty should not be sought after for its own sake. To be charitable, the selection of former senator Bob Kerrey to be the president of the New School in New York City and the choice of gallery owner Jeffrey Deitch to be the director of the Museum of Contemporary Art in Los Angeles were met with mixed reviews. Much more is needed than brand-name value. Those who search are sometimes dazzled by the shiny new object. You need to insistently ask whether the skills, background, and experience of nontraditional candidates are applicable to a brand-new environment.

Narrowing the field of candidates to those who have spent their entire lives in academia for universities, or health-care administration for hospital presidents, or philanthropic management for foundation CEOs, is a sure sign of complacency and lack of imagination. By insisting that some nontraditional prospects be seen, the hiring employer can test assumptions, try relative newcomers on for size, and determine what's best in a thorough deliberative process.

Employers and search committee members can not only set the expectation for the kind of candidate they are prepared to consider and offer specific names, they can also participate in the vetting and reference-checking process, whenever desirable.

It is worth reiterating that at every stage in the search process, care must be taken to protect its confidentiality. Candidates often do not wish their current employers to know that they are exploring alternatives. If disclosure occurs, highly desirable prospects may quickly withdraw from consideration, their reputations for candor and loyalty to their current assignments having been besmirched. Discretion and decorum must characterize search committee conduct.

**9. Has the candidate been supplied with adequate literature and documentation to conduct due diligence, to pose penetrating questions, and to offer tentative points of view?**

Assembling annual reports, operating statements, balance sheets, program literature, meeting minutes, relevant speeches, and organization charts, among other literature, will be viewed by any candidate very favorably. This vital information will inform the interview and better prepare the candidate.

*The critical clues to organizational puzzles are often readily available in written form. Too few candidates trouble to discover them. Read. Do your homework.*

*The literature provided by the employer will never tell all. But the information you have requested can often uncover important realities well worth knowing and raise questions well worth pursuing.*

**10. Is the process of vetting candidates thorough and painstaking, informing the search committee or the hiring authority about whom it is best to interview?**

After all, reference check calls originating from firms are often treated as perfunctory, or the respondent does not offer an honest assessment. When that request for complete candor comes not from a hired hand, but from a friend or a colleague who has a real stake in the outcome, uncomfortable truths are far more likely to be uncovered.

"Character is like a tree and reputation like its shadow. The shadow is what we think of it; the tree is the real thing." So said President Abraham Lincoln as he considered candidates for key positions in his administration.

Too often, employers find themselves shadowboxing, conversing in generalities and poorly sourced reputational representations.

Human beings are complex. Getting at the truth isn't easy. It requires locating those in a position to really know the candidate. It demands asking penetrating questions by those whom the interviewee trusts and respects.

The employer's objective is to identify those who know the real person and how she performs at work, formally and informally. Do not be satisfied with the shadow. Examine the tree.

**11. How well prepared are you for posing penetrating questions to the candidates, for offering forthcoming responses to their questions, and for evaluating whether a second interview should be set?**

Search committee members or interviewers must examine all written materials by and about candidates, the better to prepare themselves to ask informed questions. To avoid repetition, if a group interview is involved, members should confer with one another about the subjects each intends to cover. Some discussion of the candidate's paper credentials is in order, prior to the interview, just as postmortem conversation needs to be held immediately in its wake.

It is easy to forget key points and important to record impressions when they are fresh. Immediate feedback and exchanges of view will help to render candidate evaluation sharp and thorough.

*Have you been impressed with the knowledge and insight of those responsible for the hiring process? Have its protagonists posed questions closely connected to your background and experience? Are they people who have earned your respect? Do you believe working with them would be pleasurable and productive?*

*The answers to these questions are essential. They may well deter-mine whether you wish to continue as an applicant or to withdraw from further consideration.*

*Remember, you can call a halt to this process at any time.*

*Have you learned enough about key organizational players to con-clude that this job, in this place, at this time, is just not for you?*

## 12. Nothing justifies a longer and more time-consuming process than the search. When you near the end and still harbor doubts about the finalists, can you keep the process open to consider latecomer candidates?

Search is an exercise that involves busy people who need to dedi-cate from dozens to hundreds of hours to finding and persuad-ing the best CEO or senior officer candidate to join their favored institution.

It is time-consuming. It is taxing. It can be exhausting. Pressure mounts to reach a conclusion and call a halt to what may be, or ap-pear to be, organizational drift and uncertainty.

Sometimes the process comes to an end without the leading candidate winning the enthusiastic support of those involved in the decision. There is a sense of settling, of letting the possible become the enemy of the best. And the search firm, often eager to move on to other clients, may well encourage calling a halt to a prolonged process, implicitly or explicitly.

In such a moment of truth, when some of the search committee members believe they are about to unnecessarily compromise, sum-mon the courage to speak out. Don't mince words. State that the search needs to be reopened, that the temporary damage of delay is nothing compared to settling for a ho-hum candidate. Instead, continue to look for the very best.

Such a late-stage appeal runs the risk of offending search com-mittee colleagues who have no desire to start over and a board chair who has needed to spend additional time monitoring institutional activity without the benefit of a full-time CEO. Heavy lies the head that wears that crown.

When outsiders learn of a less-than-sterling selection and pose the question "What could they [the search committee members] have been thinking?" the answer could well be "Enough—this process must come to an end, and the sooner, the better."

The situation can be even more fraught. Board chairs and trustees are volunteers. All are expected to serve part-time. When they are busy and productive with full-time jobs and growing families, the place that trustee service plays in their lives is likely to be proportionate and balanced. As such, they have no interest in excessive involvement. Guiding policy formulation, assessing CEO performance, guarding against strategic risks to institutional welfare, protecting the mission, and strengthening the economic condition of the organization are more than enough.

Operations, broadly construed, fall to the CEO. Most trustees are looking for strength and versatility in their professional leader.

Now, consider officers of the board who once led a very active professional life and have since retired. Examine the balance of trustee leadership and ask whether, in front of titles on their biographies, is too often the modifier "former."

Such civic leaders can be ambitious for more than their traditional responsibility. They may wish to be active, even hyperactive, to burnish their reputation among peers by virtue of exemplary, high-energy, voluntary service. In a way, roles become reversed. Some trustees find that their need for a board association is greater than the organization's need for their (excessive) involvement.

The plot thickens.

Board membership is self-selected and self-perpetuating. Trustees are drawn from a pool of collective friendships and business associations, as often as not.

Under these circumstances, the social dynamic on boards of directors needs to be taken into account. It can be harmful to organizational performance.

When it comes to searches, directors or trustees who are friends of the chair, or of other influential figures, tend to defer to them reflexively. "He is my friend (or close colleague). As the chair (or senior board officer), he carries the heaviest burden of responsibility. If he seems determined to select Charlie or Harriet as the new CEO, who am I to disagree?"

Such genuflection to the chair or to a VIP endeavoring to influence the ultimate choice strikes me as an odd definition of loyalty. The best selection emerges from an open, frank, and thorough group process in which participants tell each other what they need to hear, not what they want to hear. Well-considered differences of view should be fully aired.

That is not only the proper way to discharge search responsibilities. It happens to be the truest expression of friendship.

To return to our example, if the finalist candidate falls well short of expectations, speak up. Request that the search be reopened. Ultimately the risk of institutional damage and of trustee embarrassment due to a poorly conducted or heavily compromised search can be very high. Being complicit in an unfortunate choice turns out to be hardly a favor to that board friend you did not wish to oppose. After all, his or her reputation is in play, far more than your own.

### 13. During the search, are you sufficiently aware of the need to persuade candidates about this exciting career opportunity as much as to judge them?

Talent is scarce. Securing it for your organization is a highly competitive process. The searching employer must keep in mind that while initially you hold all of the cards in determining who receives the hiring offer, there is a delicate moment when the tables are turned.

From the inception of the search, its members need to anticipate that the time will come when they are no longer in the catbird seat. How persuasively they interpret the mission of the organization, how enthusiastically they pledge fidelity to a new and exciting set of aspirations, and how stylistically they have treated the candidate will weigh heavily in the outcome.

The applicant who successfully competed for the job now must determine whether she really wants it. Assuming salary, benefits, and other terms and conditions of employment are within acceptable range, are the trustees and staff people with whom the candidate wishes to work? "Is this new assignment worth uprooting myself and my family from our existing circumstances, compared to what other alternatives I might consider? Indeed, if I disclose the new offer to my current employer, might it, in an effort to keep me, seek to provide a much better package of compensation and other benefits than what I currently enjoy?"

*Let's assume you have taken the next step. You have agreed to a second and final interview.*

*If you are now dubious about developing sound partnerships with key members of a board, respect that judgment. Consider it a strong warning sign.*

*If you believe that some organizational leaders are too dominating, opinionated, or aggressive, now is the time to reconsider.*

*Remember, it is easy to be lured into a situation that may well not be the best one for you.*

*Search committee members are wooing you. Compliments fly across the conference room. Suddenly, praise knows few bounds.*

*I am reminded of what Adlai Stevenson once said of flattery. "It's just like smoking. Harmless, but only if you do not inhale."*

*Instead, exhale. The moment of truth is upon you.*

**14. As the final decision approaches and you are about to extend an offer, have you formulated a plan B if, for whatever reasons, it is declined?**

The more attractive the candidate you are pursuing, the more likely he or she can exercise other options.

In search committee deliberations, it is important to answer the what-if question.

What if your first choice declines your offer?

Then what?

Has your search been conducted in a manner broad enough and deep enough to have unearthed more than one very attractive contender?

**15. At what point are one or two successful candidates exposed to an authority like the full board of directors or the CEO for final approval?**

When the search committee or senior interviewer is satisfied that the best available candidate has been identified, an introduction to the board or the CEO should happen as quickly as possible. Except on the rarest of occasions, only the preferred finalist should be presented, with the second candidate held in reserve, just in case the unexpected occurs. Perhaps the recommended candidate either surprisingly withdraws or is somehow rejected by the ultimate decision maker.

Well-performing organizations are comfortable in delegating authority to duly constituted committees. In unhealthy, dysfunctional organizations, the largest group of trustees comprise the Committee on Second-Guessing. Assuming that the trust invested in members of a diligent, well-selected search committee is returned by engaging the balance of the board's general views and informing trustees of progress regularly, then, in most cases, this streamlined and expeditious method of proceeding will be entirely acceptable.

**16. Has ample consideration been given to the economic needs and family circumstances of the candidate?**

Negotiating an acceptable letter of agreement should be delegated to a single board member, a trustee attorney, or a small compensation committee possessed of an agreed-upon range of discretionary authority.

No prudent nonprofit or corporation wishes to be less than forthcoming with its new CEO or senior officer on often complex and delicate issues.

The start date? Assistance in finding an appropriate professional position for a trailing spouse? Tuition subsidy for kids in private school? A housing allowance?

These and other issues of compensation can best be judged in the context of having benchmarked the practices of similarly situated institutions. If a study by a reputable firm specializing in executive compensation has not recently been commissioned, then the search committee should arrange for one in anticipation of its new hire. What other institutional analogues are doing may not be dispositive of every question that arises, but they do provide a measure of assurance that the compensation package under consideration is not an outlier or a potential source of institutional embarrassment. Such a formal report is also useful in responding to any inquiries from the federal government, like the Internal Revenue Service, or from the state government, like the attorney general.

### 17. Does the letter of agreement include a provision that sets forth an expectation of annual evaluation of CEO performance based on articulated measurable objectives?

The failure to formalize a process for assessing a CEO is a major cause of institutional breakdown, paralysis, and drift. The search committee's job is not done when the leading candidate is identified, recommended, and approved. Its members can not yet fully exhale.

Whoever is hired needs to understand from the outset that the board expects a well-defined process of objective setting, benchmarking, and performance evaluation to be established for assessing CEO and institutional performance. The outcome requires widespread board consensus and approval.

## 18. Is the hiring group or individual prepared to support the winning candidate on the one hand, and to assign a designated set of trustees to objectively evaluate performance on the other?

It is a source of amazement that boards of directors do not uniformly and consistently insist on the development by the CEO of annual measurable objectives. Once reviewed, modified, and approved, this statement becomes a critical assessment tool through which the CEO is held accountable for institutional performance. It plays a major role in determining whether a salary is increased or a bonus conferred, and the amount.

The annual review of performance against stated measurable objectives gives the trustees or directors the opportunity to offer praise or criticism with a view toward continuous improvement.

Importantly, if the CEO falls well shy of meeting agreed-upon targets, then an objective predicate for discharge, or compelled resignation, will have been established.

It is extremely helpful if the hiring authority sets a firm deadline for the crafting of an operating set of performance metrics. Otherwise, this fundamental requisite of sound management and monitoring runs the risk of not materializing.

Only the discipline of consistent operational review permits an assessment of CEO performance that is fair, thorough, and well understood by all concerned parties.

It objectifies how the CEO is doing and discards many of the irrelevant observations that could otherwise fill the vacuum. Whether the CEO is liked by trustees and directors. Whether he or she "manages up" well. Whether articulation of institutional purpose is eloquent. These are all no substitute for operational excellence and for the delivery of expected results.

Such a plan also protects search committee members whose own egos may be much too invested in the CEO selection. Often, they have a difficult time judging whether that choice is, in fact, working. It is healthy for the group that recommended a leader to wish that new incumbent every success. It is quite another matter for members of the search committee to become blind adherents to their chosen CEO. Institutions need empathic, supportive trustees and directors. They do not need ego-driven cheerleaders. They need least of all an amen chorus.

What well-wishers on the board can do is to help the new leader plan and execute a successful transition.

Properly communicating the announcement to all key stakeholders in writing. Helping the new CEO or senior executive meet with important internal and external parties: investors, partners, suppliers, government officials, journalists, trustees or directors, predecessors, and others in a position to offer sound advice and guidance. Organizing social events where meeting, greeting, mixing, and mingling can occur comfortably in group settings. Well executed, these tasks and occasions can help minimize the number of time-consuming one-on-one sessions required for the new appointee.

Some organizations arrange for an overlap in service between the incumbent and the successor. If the outgoing and incoming executives are compatible, the newcomer may well benefit from a period of orientation and learning freed of having to assume immediate operational responsibilities.

Finally, the trustees can offer honest views about institutional priorities and worrisome pitfalls. The period immediately after the appointment is a critical time for you to build trust and to treat the CEO fully as an insider.

These are the kinds of initiatives you, as the welcoming authorities (at whose pleasure the CEO serves), and senior executives, can take to help launch the new leader. Such onboarding exercises can ease the transition process and reduce uncertainty and anxiety.

*Well, did this whole process demonstrate enough to help you address those three fundamental questions with which we began? After all of this dating, are you still willing to become engaged to the target employer? If a professional marriage proposal is forthcoming and the dowry, in the form of your compensation package, is acceptable, are nuptials in your future? Or, even at this very late stage, do you decide to leave that potential employer at the altar?*

*It's your life. It's your call.*

## Some Searches That Matter Most
## (To Me)

Recruiting, motivating, training, assessing, recognizing, and rewarding high-performing professionals is the best method of retaining them.

It is the pathway to institutional success. It is well worth repeating that the worst time to find a superior executive is when you need one.

But when those circumstances do arise, what can be more compelling than filling that critical vacancy with the best-qualified candidate?

Is there an episode in the life of an organization more galvanizing than the search for a CEO who can lead it successfully, or for a senior officer to assume responsibility for mission-critical activities?

With all of this being widely recognized rhetorically, why, then, do employers so frequently perform poorly through some combination of avoidance and neglect?

How can so many search committees fail to select successful CEOs? Why do so many organizations fall short in designing effective succession plans? In their absence, generating excellent internal candidates to fill vacancies, including those of the most senior managers, is virtually impossible. What role do search firms play in this selection process and how can their track record be fundamentally improved?

At the 92nd Street Y, where I served as executive director for eight years, my two board-selected successors each departed the premises in about eighteen months. My immediate predecessor in that post had been fired unceremoniously a little more than a single year after being retained.

Three decades later, at Lincoln Center, where I served for thirteen years, it was déjà vu all over again. The CEO I replaced had lasted only nine months on the job, and the presidents who succeeded me lasted twenty-seven and twelve months, respectively. In between these changes of leadership, there were prolonged inter-regna with new searches needing to be organized and completed.

The consequences? Institutional drift. Employee confusion. Passivity. Risk aversion. Talent loss. Mounting deficits.

But at AT&T, both successors to me as the president of the AT&T Foundation were well-prepared internal candidates. They performed admirably. At the International Rescue Committee, my successor as president, George Rupp, chosen after a lengthy and deliberative board search, offered outstanding service for over a decade. And the current incumbent, David Miliband, has been acquitting himself with distinction under very trying external circumstances, generally inimical to refugees and asylum seekers. As a result, institutional momentum has been maintained, desirable staff remain on board, and missions are being accomplished.

What accounts for the difference?

Why are tributes to the importance of human resources so often empty and ritualistic?

For when the need arises, the competition for attracting and retaining superior employees has never been as fierce.

What is it about your business setting that can most attract talented executives and keep them motivated, productive, and enjoying their work? What kind of firm or organization are you trying to build that will help you persuade a world-class employee to fill that critical vacancy?

Ultimately, the hunt for the best-in-class staff is more than a competition for talent. Rather, it is identifying anew the role of the organization and what you wish it to accomplish in the future. For customers. For investors. For suppliers. For community partners. For shareowners. And, of course, for highly valued employees.

Here are the steps wise employers need to consider as they enter the toughest and most forbidding marketplace, looking to compete successfully for adroit leaders to join them.

## The Competition for Talent: Keys to Success

1. If you don't know in which direction your organization should be traveling, any CEO can lead it there. First, define institutional goals and priorities with care. Then, look for the leader who can pave the way to realizing them.

2. It is far easier and less costly to retain a high-performing senior executive than to replace one.

3. To avoid searching outside for talent, look right around you. Outstanding leaders may be hiding in plain sight.

4. Building a pipeline of proficient leaders in your organization requires a process to identify and invest in them. Recognize, reward, praise, and nurture these precious human resources. They are nothing less than your organization's future.

5. Choose a search firm using a rigorous process and manage its performance tightly.

6. In filling vacancies, select, do not settle.

7. As you screen candidates, shun confirmation bias. Listen carefully. Check references extensively and rigorously.

8. The greater the number of parties involved in a search, the more likely confusion will ensue and privacy will be compromised.

9. Limit the number of encounters a candidate needs to undergo. Multiple meetings can be discordant and time-consuming. Search processes need deadlines. They do not age well. But it is far better to delay in the interest of selecting a superior candidate than to end on time having settled on an uninspiring, lackluster option.

10. Employers must do more than identify and select talented candidates to recruit. They must successfully woo them.

11. For want of resourcefulness, a preferred candidate can be lost. Be flexible in negotiating terms and conditions of employment.

12. If possible, plan for some overlap between the effective hiring date of the successor and the departure date of the incumbent. Such a transitional period of weeks or months can prove invaluable.

13. Plan for a comprehensive, bespoke onboarding process for the new hire. It should embrace disciplined reading and meetings with key institutional stakeholders, not least employees and all members of the board of directors.

14. Be clear. The CEO manages; the board governs. The CEO proposes; the board disposes.

15. Expect to receive within ninety days of hire a statement of objectives and anticipated key results, with clear deadlines. Hold its author accountable for achieving them and appraise performance accordingly.

16. Provide well-sourced feedback to the new hire. Executive performance should be an exercise in continuous improvement. Through careful inquiry and sensitive scrutiny, help inform that process with candid conversation.

# -7-

# **Performance**

## Excelling at Work

---

*"To learn means to accept the postulate that life did not begin at my birth. Others have been there before me, and I walk in their footsteps."*

—Elie Wiesel

*"Ability is what you're capable of. Motivation determines what you do. Attitude determines how well you do it."*
—Lou Holtz, legendary football coach at Notre Dame[1]

If and when the congratulatory call comes, offering you that job, the very one you have competed for over many months, do not accept immediately. Yes, you will be sorely tempted. The salary and fringe benefit package proposed will then be wrapped in blandishment and tied up in a ribbon conveying what may appear, or what is intended to be, a take-it-or-leave-it package.

And, by now, you will be eager to let others know of your appointment and start working in your new post.

Don't do it.

Instead, offer warm thanks, listen carefully to the terms and conditions of proposed employment, request them in writing, and express enthusiasm about reviewing and discussing the specifics in the days immediately ahead.

After all, now is the time when you, as the sought-after executive, enjoy maximum leverage. Given all that you have been through with the search firm, the search committee, the reactions to your likely written statements, the reference checks, and the delays in arranging meetings, holding your future employer at bay for a while is only fair play.

Think about the offer. Talk to your partner at home and your closest friends. Sleep on it.

Go back to basics. Ask yourself, knowing what you now know, do you really want that job for which you have competed successfully?

> Criteria for choosing what's next may be based on available resources (proximity, time, money), coherence (how the alternative fits into your Lifeview and Workview), your confidence level (do you believe you can do this?) and how much you like it.[2]

Assuming this fresh look at the new opportunity still leaves you sanguine, then examine with care the content of the proposed terms and conditions of employment.

Salary and bonus? Term of service? Start date? Special arrangements for a trailing professional spouse? Housing allowance? Reimbursement for relocation costs? Class of travel, on the ground and in the air? Compensation for any earned benefits you might be relinquishing when you leave your current post? Arrangements for the next review of compensation, its timing and its process?

As you accept a first job offer or any subsequent one, do not sell yourself short when the subject turns to salary and benefits.

Once you become formally employed, all kinds of limitations on compensation increases and bonuses are likely to come into play. Human resource departments and boards of directors may establish tight guidelines and firm rules governing such matters. Their application to varying circumstances is often widely and rightly seen to be arbitrary and unfair.

As a new employee, eagerly awaited by your soon-to-be boss, the opportunity to negotiate with a more willing and accommodating party may never be as promising. Take full advantage of it.

Overcome a natural reluctance to specify a higher figure as a starting salary that you would welcome. Hopefully, required IRS filings, websites like Glassdoor, and conversations with employees to whom you are introduced can provide some sense of the competitive compensation range.

Here are a few lines that can help you move from hesitancy to being explicit.

> I am really looking forward to joining the firm and working at your side. I intend to give this job my all. And I'd be grateful if you could see your way to a [fill in the blank] starting salary with the opportunity to earn a year-end performance bonus of [fill in the blank] consistent with the proven value I will bring to the organization.

Now suppose the reply states that this position carries a top pay and bonus short of what you requested. Of course, you can accept it with no questions asked. But if money is important to you, then why not ask to split the difference. "Can we shake hands on meeting halfway?"

Take my word for it. No one will think less of you for having tried. Particularly so if your tone of voice is serious, relaxed, honest, and earnest.

Exhibiting self-assurance in the value you bring to the firm should continue throughout your employment up to and including becoming a CEO. As you are considered for salary increases or special bonuses, take the occasion in meetings and in writing to state what you believe you deserve.

When your boss informs you of the decision, express genuine thanks, but don't hesitate to ask questions like:

Can I be confident that no one in the firm holding a position like mine and contributing comparably to its success is treated more generously in salary and target bonus?

Are you personally comfortable that this offer is fair and forthcoming?

Might we spend a little time discussing ways in which I can offer added value in the year ahead so as to justify consideration for a promotion and/or more generous compensation as we look forward together?

Now is the time to suggest additional roles you can play in the organization, or work products you can deliver, or training courses in which you are more than willing to enroll.

However the discussion ends, commit to writing your appreciation for the time and consideration offered. Use that email or letter to summarize the assurances you received in response to the questions just posed.

At a minimum, these conversations and the expressions of intent you have dutifully recorded enhance mutual understanding and appreciation. Carefully and gracefully worded, they will be well received.

Should for any reason acrimony and arbitrary treatment surface, you will then have a written contemporaneous record of what your employer stated and intended. It can be used to appeal the latest decision about compensation to higher authority.

In extreme cases, you will have created a well-timed documentary account on the partial basis of which you can have a claim mediated, arbitrated, or litigated.

While this advice is applicable to all, I especially hope women will act on it. In a lifetime of experience, playing many roles and monitoring many others in a wide variety of workplaces, I have concluded that women tend to outperform men. They are generally more methodical. More team and results oriented. More willing to give credit to others for success. More self-aware.

Humble and hardworking, women frequently demur when praise is directed their way. They often understate their contributions to project success. The team is invoked and credit for accomplishment is attributed to the group as a whole. Not surprisingly, then, when salary and promotion issues are weighed and resolved, women are less forthcoming about what they deserve and more willing to accept what is offered on the spot. Don't be diffident or self-effacing. Take a deep breath and unflinchingly ask for what you deserve. Timidity and nervousness win you no credit at the workplace. Instead, to borrow a phrase, lean in to the process of decision making on reward and recognition and ask for what you think is fair and meritorious.[3]

Closing the gap between how women and men are paid and promoted is primarily the responsibility of honorable and savvy employers. But there is no harm in helping the organization you work for to reach that destination.

And for those men whose personalities leave them less than compelling and persuasive in their own negotiating, listen up. This encouragement is intended for you as well.

In essence, be sure that you are comfortable with all material compensation matters. It is important that you feel treated equitably. If your employer is excessively rigid about terms and conditions at the outset, what sort of message are you being sent and what is the likely environment that you will encounter when you arrive on the scene? Conversely, do not be seen as attempting to extract every last dollar before you sign on the dotted line. A too-tough stance could well be viewed as unseemly.

Hopefully, an acceptable compromise can be crafted quickly. When that happens, here is what I have suggested as general guidance for that first year in your new position as CEO or as a senior executive.

## Leadership Dos and Don'ts

One of the most common and misleading pieces of advice offered to organizational leaders is to begin wholesale change quickly. Discharge mediocre, underperforming employees or those resisting your leadership. Hire new staff who prize loyalty to you above all, preferably those who have worked at your side in the past. Announce new initiatives to signify a brisk departure from prior practice.

This "act first, act now, listen later," top-down approach to major institutional change rarely works. It triggers opposition. It spreads insecurity and worry throughout the organization. It leads to accusations of arbitrary and capricious behavior on the part of a novice, know-it-all senior executive. It cripples morale. Who is s/he to take that step so soon? What does s/he really know?[4]

Moving too quickly, except in the case of a genuine emergency, rarely works for the organization or for the newcomer. Instead, become an insider. Listen carefully and purposefully to trustees, staff, and important figures in a position to support the organization. Lift expectations for individual and collective performance. Raise the metabolism of the place. Lead by example. Arrive early. Leave late. Exhibit energy, curiosity, empathy, and optimism. Emphasize steady, incremental progress and connect its achievement to employee incentives and recognition. Respect your colleagues.

Do all of that and watch what happens. Employees who can't keep pace with activity and higher standards begin to leave of their own accord. They can be replaced with more energetic and ambitious newcomers who help to change the institutional culture. Momentum builds. Some incumbents actually change their habits and get with the program. It can all occur naturally and organically. The pace of change is deliberate. The CEO allows for time to reach decisions intelligently, to develop new information and to course correct. Employees learn what is expected of them. The critical mass of the organization must be in agreement and in alignment if ambitious goals are to be realized.[5]

Aim to create an environment in which gifted employees all around you can do their best work.

Remove obstacles to achieving excellent results. Stamp out cumbersome review processes. Streamline rules of all kinds. Call a halt to creeping bureaucracy. Offer praise to your colleagues, whenever merited, privately and publicly. Be willing to weed out poor performers after ample discussion and proper notice.

Steer clear of being driven by your in-box. But don't entirely ignore what lands there. For in it you will find the trivial and the important, the urgent and the many items that are hardly time sensitive. Try to determine what you wish to accomplish each day. Give those items preference over the steady stream of requests, demands, and information that come your way. Importantly, set aside time to think, reflect, and read. And be open to ideas and information generated internally and externally. There are very intelligent people inside and outside your place of work who wish to convey what they know to you. Do not discourage them. Your constant challenge is to separate the wheat from the chaff.

Positively facilitate outstanding performance. Provide the resources needed for colleagues to realize superior results. Ample budget allotments. Adequate time to complete projects. The right number and kind of personnel. Offers of other material and psychic support.

Encourage leaders throughout the organization to emulate these action steps. Reduce the inhibitors and increase the accelerants to team success.

When in doubt about what promising employees most need, ask them.

None of this is simple.

Overcoming an organizational immune system accustomed to resisting innovation and change requires persistent and measured pressure. It rarely happens quickly, or dramatically, without the senior executive encountering countervailing opposition.

But once a healthy process is set in motion and once the credibility and self-confidence of a leader is established, it is then possible to oust employees who actively resist changes in direction and clear accountability. Staff inclined to dig in their heels and cling to past ways of doing business will feel more and more isolated. Discharging them after well-documented trial periods and after their demonstrated failures to meet clear, agreed-upon objectives rarely evokes much protest. Patience, determination, and fairness are what's in order in dealing with especially difficult employees or malcontents.

At Lincoln Center, the search committee members who recommended that I be hired knew that there were many challenges to be addressed, but they were also justifiably proud of what they and their colleagues had accomplished. Indeed, two of the search committee members, Nat Leventhal, my predecessor once removed, and Beverly Sills, the first chair of the board, with whom I needed to work closely, were both largely responsible for many achievements as well as for a state of affairs that called for change.

By necessity, such change occasionally meant altering what they had created and dismantling what they had built. Proceeding too quickly could easily have been viewed as a repudiation of much of their legacy. Instead, mutual trust had to be developed. Positive experiences together needed to be shared. Generous acknowledgment of the achievements of predecessors was warmly welcomed as well. Then, and only then, could recommendations for change be judged on the merits. Then, and only then, were those responsible for the status quo likely to be more receptive to change. They became allies and supporters rather than sources of dissent and steadfast defenders of the then state of affairs.

Treat your predecessors as mentors, ask for their advice, consult with them as you reach critical decisions. The tendency to act as if organizational life began with your arrival is not only naive; it can be fatal. There is plenty to learn from those who came before you. And, if for any reason, your predecessors abstain, well, no one will blame you for having failed to try. Besides, others on staff or on the board of directors who are familiar with institutional history and its lessons are available for advice and counsel.

While you are taking these steps, developing expectations and aligning them, designing key elements of your strategy and working to improve the organizational culture, do not neglect to keep your boss or the board well informed.

There are so many internal and external forces at work, so many issues and personalities to manage, that you run the risk of taking for granted those from whom you derive authority.

Be sure you communicate early and often with everyone who holds you accountable for overall institutional performance. Phone calls and email are essential. But there is nothing as important as regular meetings to process business and to build relationships. Put them on your calendar. Make them happen.

Perhaps most important, communicate your objectives and overall agenda frequently. In all-staff meetings and in small groups. At full board meetings and in committee sessions. Use every opportunity to be sure that these gatherings do not become forums for one-way communication. Listen carefully to what is being said. Closely observe the reactions, verbal and unspoken.

Do not closet yourself away from those whose very cooperation is vital to realizing the firm's mission. Self-imposed isolation leads to rumor, speculation, and worry. It can spread throughout the organization and quickly.

Justice Brandeis was right. Sunlight is the best disinfectant.

Illuminate what you are about and how important it is for others to join you by conforming their agenda to your own and the converse. After all, what you are setting forth was influenced, in no small measure, by many of the very employees to whom you are now appealing. Your agenda should have been formed in large part by the information and perspectives gathered during your trustee and staff listening tours.

Well, here's the thing.

According to public reports and private accounts from dozens of insiders, my two immediate successors at Lincoln Center adhered to very few of these general pieces of management advice. Their performance was breathtakingly deficient. I doubt that either

troubled to take advantage of the written experience of my tenure
as the president of Lincoln Center. Apparently, it did not occur to
them that my inscribed gift copy to each of *They Told Me Not to
Take That Job: Tumult, Betrayal, Heroics, and the Transformation of
Lincoln Center*[6] was intended for their reading, not their shelving.

I wish that I had been given a comparable written distillation of
the experience of my predecessor, not to mention a possible guide
to my first year in office! Neither the book nor any other circumstances prompted either of them to ask me a single question.

Their lack of interest in contacting me to request briefings or
respond to inquiries of any kind was regrettable. Apparently, they
did not know of, or take much stock in, William Faulkner's observation that "The past is never dead. It's not even past."[7] In this act
of omission, they are hardly alone.

Listen to the extraordinarily successful two-time governor of
California, the former mayor of Oakland, the former state attorney general, and the former Democratic Party chairman of California, Jerry Brown. After concluding his last eight successful years
as governor, highlighted by Brown inheriting a $26 billion deficit
and leaving a $14 billion surplus for a $40 billion turnaround, here
is what this experience-rich politician had to say on the subject. In
a farewell interview with Adam Nagourney of the *New York Times*,
when asked about whether his Democratic successor as governor
had sought his counsel, Brown offered an unvarnished response:

> No one has ever asked me for advice. No one. Ever. I am one of the
> most knowledgeable people in American politics and no one has ever
> asked. Not even local candidates. They don't do that. Politicians are
> surrounded by [their own] consultants and staff.[8]

And so it was at Lincoln Center. Evidently, my two immediate
successors felt no need to inquire after any aspect of leading a complex place from someone who had done so for thirteen years, arguably with more than a modicum of success. Their severely curtailed

tenure proved otherwise and much faster than anyone expected, least of all them. Each was exited quickly, the first in twenty-seven months, the second in twelve. Neither merits a footnote in Lincoln Center's storied history.

Fortunately, Russell Granet, a very talented insider, was then appointed acting president. He brought calmness, stability, and a sense of direction to an institution reeling from so many changes at the top. Now the CEO of the New 42nd Street, Russell was succeeded by Henry Timms, effective in May 2019. Henry became Lincoln Center's president after a successful tenure as executive director of the 92nd Street Y. It comes with a considerable sense of relief to learn that Henry has been very well received in the early months of his service. So far, so good. All who care about Lincoln Center's future wish him an accomplishment-filled tenure.

If at the top of the institutional ladder is the CEO from whom we should expect superior performance, what of all the line executives and support staff?

In my judgment, nothing is better than possessing knowledge and skills that your employer finds invaluable.[9] Your pursuit of excellence will require months and years of deliberate work. Read, study, practice, and consult with authorities in your field. Malcolm Gladwell puts the number of required hours for mastery at no fewer than ten thousand in his book *Outliers*.[10] Excelling demands a commitment to continuous improvement and a willingness to subject your work to the critique of others, including colleagues playing the roles of mentor and coach.

If you are acknowledged to be a practitioner consistently delivering your highest and best talent to advance a firm's mission, little else matters. Of course, it is assumed that professional excellence needs to be combined with ethical integrity, strong interpersonal skills, the proclivity to fit in the organization's culture, and the capacity to work well in teams. Performance shortfalls on these key dimensions explain why university leaders so often fail, according to *Presidencies Derailed*.[11] The authors put the reasons for failure in the form of questions that will seem familiar to any who observed Lincoln Center's recent experience with its own derailed CEOs.

> Why would a new president request [the functional equivalent of] letters of resignation from all senior staff so that she may decide who stays and who goes?
> Why would a new president not start by sitting down personally with major stakeholder groups?
> Why would a new president...fall prey to the temptations of power?
> Why would a new president not take the time to learn the culture of an institution before taking up a broom, shovel and wrench to make wholesale changes?

These leading questions apply not just to the CEO, but to all managers within an institution.

## Moving Up, Gracefully

For everyone, I'd encourage conceiving of your role at work broadly, not narrowly.

If you have the energy to offer your boss or colleagues the time to help on a project that may need additional personnel, or to suggest an initiative not now on the organization's agenda, then by all means volunteer your services. If the offer is accepted, the broader range of responsibility will have others viewing you as someone with knowledge and skills that extend beyond your current position in the firm. Knowing of the added value you can bring to other assignments increases the likelihood that you will be asked to broaden your job description. The odds of your moving more quickly to a promotion also improve.

Even if your offer is declined, you will be credited by your boss and peers with being a team player.

Two instances come to mind during my longest full-time stint as a president. First, the director of Lincoln Center's facilities figured out precisely how our sixteen acres could physically accommodate Fashion Week, which had been lodged at Bryant Park for seventeen consecutive years and was looking to relocate. Its logistical requirements were complex and daunting. Second, the chief financial officer of Lincoln Center worked closely with Channel 13 and the Big Apple Circus so that the former could become a long-term tenant of Lincoln Center on the corner of Sixty-Sixth Street and Broadway and the latter could remain at Damrosch Park. Neither assignment was easy or straightforward. These were extraordinary examples of exceptional service.

Such accomplishments left a positive impression with all of their colleagues, not least me.

In many organizations employees can feel stuck, confined unduly and for too long to one department and to the same set of responsibilities, narrowly interpreted. Boredom seeps into their day-to-day working life. Don't let that condition prevail.

Instead, volunteer to help, cheerfully and enthusiastically. Be seen as someone who wishes colleagues to succeed. By assisting them to do so, you will learn a great deal about your own and other organizational units, and you will develop an internal network of admiring, grateful associates.

While I strongly encourage taking initiatives and stretching your management and leadership skills, there are several warnings to consider heeding as you seek to broaden what you learn, who you meet and how you can be most useful.

First, be sure that your current responsibilities are being fully discharged. Avoid being seen as someone straying from a formal assignment, your "day job," to freelance in other areas.

Second, spend most time staying in your lane. Straying too often suggests an overzealousness and may incur the antagonism of others who understandably are protective of their turf.

In extending an offer to others, or taking an initiative only after receiving authorization, the chances that you will be viewed as encroaching on the territory of colleagues are minimized. By positioning yourself in a support role and crediting your colleagues with accomplishment, you will be regarded as someone who cares more about results than about personal advancement.

Most of the time, it is the workhorses and not the show horses who enjoy the brightest professional future.

Beyond developing deep expertise in the subject matter and perfecting your craft, look all around you. Like the graduate student pursuing a dual-degree program, let your natural curiosity wander into adjacent fields. If you are in product development, ask colleagues about how you can learn more about sales and marketing. If you are assigned to external communications, explore how your government relations counterparts approach their work. Draft a speech for a senior executive as if it had been assigned to you. Outline a marketing opportunity you detect as if doing so were your responsibility. Share these with relevant colleagues. Offer up your work product with humility, even anonymity. Seek their reactions.

By cultivating informal networks within a firm, you better prepare yourself for broader responsibility and inform current job performance.

And take full advantage of the formal learning and training opportunities offered by your employer. They may involve in-house educational programs, online offerings, two- and three-week gatherings of professionals on a college campus drawn from many companies, other opportunities to improve professional practice, and even subsidies to study not just for certificates of course completion, but for advanced degrees. Increasingly, employers are willing to invest in you by offsetting the high cost of such offerings with generous financial support.

Seek out the colleagues you admire and ask for a little time to converse. Over breakfast, lunch, or just a cup of coffee. Ask them how they learned their craft, who served as their mentors, and what is now on their recommended reading list. Inquire about their professional journeys and whether there are stops along the way that you might wish to more deeply explore: places, people, concepts.

The idea is not to leave your current employer while remonstrating with yourself. Avoid fretting over what you could have done, might have done, or would have done. Instead, exploit as many of the formal and informal sources of valuable information and perspective as you can find.

In essence, when you move out to another position or move up in your current place of employment, do so without regretting having missed chances to earn and learn in tandem.

Those with whom you seek an audience and from whom you request advice are likely to be flattered. They may even enroll in your fan club.

# – 8 –

# Ready, Set

---

*"Nothing will ever be attempted, if all possible objections must first be overcome."*

—Samuel Johnson[1]

*"Believe you can, and you're halfway there."*

—Theodore Roosevelt[2]

The enemy of career development is inertia. When in doubt, act, reflect, learn, and repeat. Do not allow yourself to drift, procrastinate, or become morose in the face of setbacks. Rarely is the process of securing a desirable post as fast, straightforward, or pleasant as you would like. Being selected for a prized position is almost always a marathon, not a sprint. If you are suddenly thrust into a job search, it may well take between nine months and a year to land well.

In today's swiftly changing employment market, the laws of physics apply with vengeance: a body at rest tends to stay at rest, and a body in motion tends to stay in motion.

The tendency to hesitate, to overthink whether to place that phone call, read that pertinent article or book, dash off that email, or set up that breakfast date is debilitating. Temporizing and delaying closes you off from new ideas, new connections, and reunions with important friends and acquaintances. You run the risk of having them drift away. Remember, opportunities are out there, eager for you to find them. They are not at the desk of your current employer or at your kitchen table, seeking discovery.

Ask yourself, what am I waiting for? Do not let the best of circumstances be the enemy of the good or the good of the possible. What is the cost/benefit of action versus inaction? In looking for the next professional step, she who hesitates is lost. Because the worst that can happen when you ask for help is that you receive a negative reply, or none at all. On occasion, your request for assistance will be rejected or ignored. So what? Be resilient. Bounce back. Move on.

As I reflect on my career, the mistakes I committed were more acts of omission than commission. When I faltered, I failed to follow my instincts. I did not commit an idea to paper. I neglected to warn my boss about operational risks that might not have been obvious or immediate. I did not take the initiative and pursue that part-time job in teaching, or consulting, or writing. I lost touch with current or former colleagues and, therefore, with their network of relationships.

Like the tennis player who keeps moving in anticipation of a return volley or the chess player who thinks many moves ahead, you must commit yourself to being part of the action for as long as it takes. Often, professional alternatives surface as the result of the questions you pose to friends and acquaintances. Do not fail to ask them. Do not fret about imposing. Those who feel uncomfortable will tell you so.

Remember, most desirable jobs are likely to be filled by a candidate who is a trusted colleague or friend of the employer. The cold circulation of résumés or the response to anonymous postings rarely engenders a positive response.

Do not deprive those in your extended network of choosing to help you. Its members will feel much better for doing so. Particularly if you express gratitude, reporting from time to time on your progress and reiterating your thanks.

Maintaining visibility assumes many forms. Let's recapitulate just some of them.

- Meeting and greeting others at social occasions.

- Volunteering for civic, nonprofit, or political causes.

- Participating in alumni and alumnae activities harking back to elementary and secondary school, college, and graduate school.

- Speaking publicly at the Rotary, the Young Presidents' Organization (YPO), or other professional associations.

- Writing for print publications, social media, or blogs.

- Appearing on television, radio, or podcasts.

- Taking on special assignments at work.

- Traveling, whenever the opportunity presents itself.

- Mixing and mingling with the parents of your child's classmates.

- Accepting part-time assignments while you look for a fresh full-time post.

From any and all of these activities, you are likely to find yourself less than six degrees of separation from a coveted opening.

Personally, I never thought much about the components of my existing network, let alone about how best to strengthen it. I just naturally met a lot of professionals from different backgrounds and occupations and maintained contact with them. But the detailed techniques involved in expanding and improving that network are well worth your serious consideration. Once built, how best to utilize its members for coaching while in a job, and for market intelligence to find and secure the next one are valuable skills to acquire. Reid Hoffman, the co-founder of LinkedIn, and Ben Casnocha

have given serious thought to career transformation and the actionable intelligence that leads you there. Of all of the how-to books
I have encountered, theirs, *The Start-Up of You*, is most valuable
for its focus on the best paths to self-realization in tomorrow's
economy.[3]

## Leaping Over the Hurdles to Networking

Even assuming you accept the importance of circulating, of getting
out there, of making your presence felt, there are often barriers to
overcome, real and self-imposed.

Like me, you may be naturally shy. Like me, you may not easily remember the names of others. Like me, casual chitchat,
water-cooler conversation, might not come easily.

The best way for me to meet people and come to know them
better is to learn enough in advance so as to be able to pose intelligent questions and to engage them in active discussion.

Of course, you can always resort to asking the banker, the private
equity manager, or the retail department store executive, "How's
business?" I suspect the response to such a broad question will be
short and unlikely to generate much further conversation.

But what if you knew enough to ask the banker what he thought
of the prospects for the Federal Reserve Board raising or lowering
interest rates in the year ahead and by how much, how soon? And
then ask, how would that answer be likely to affect his business?

What if you knew enough to ask the private equity manager
whether the major challenge ahead is raising the next round of
funding or investing the firm's existing dry powder?

Just suppose that you inquired of the retail executive about the
interaction between internet and store sales. What is the relative
proportion of click and brick purchase and in which direction is it
moving?

Such questions are the pathway to overcoming shyness and your
possible discomfort with just shooting the breeze.

As for not remembering people, why not just self-confidently approach that "nameless" person with an outstretched right hand and say, "Hi. I am so-and-so. Really glad to see you again."

Most of the time, the response will be a warm and friendly greeting. More than likely you will be pleased to hear by way of response, "Of course, I remember you. I'm Sue."

And then you are off to the conversational races.

So overcome any shyness and aversion to small talk. As with any other matter, by practicing how to engage others, the process will come more naturally. Soon, you will be enjoying the experience, remembering names more frequently, not being flummoxed when you fail to, and readily engaging in discussion with veritable strangers.

## Professional Renewal

Looking for another job is probably a lot easier when you are in one compared to when you are unemployed and without a base of operations. You may be motivated to leave your current job because the path to advancement is blocked, or because there are just too many bureaucratic or personality conflicts at work. You could be worn down. You might also feel overworked, underpaid, and underappreciated. There may be less and less to learn and few, if any, colleagues left to admire. Tellingly, lassitude may have set in at a workplace you have come to dread.

Still, pushing off from your current position to your next one has a great deal to commend itself. You probably have access to an associate who can answer phone calls, a place to receive mail and email, and a professional home to talk about, even tout. If you can bring yourself to tolerate your job long enough to locate and land another, so much the better.

But some people find it difficult to juggle working full-time, managing responsibilities at home, *and* earnestly searching for another post.

They need a break in their routine. They feel compelled to free themselves from current work obligations to think more clearly about their future. Remaining in a setting from which they wish to escape may mean looking too often in the rearview mirror. For them, it is time to move on.

If this description fits your condition and if you are able psychologically and economically to leave your current position, then planning a transition between full-time assignments can be highly desirable.

First, try to arrange a separation from your current firm on favorable financial terms with a bonus, severance, and health benefits secured for as long as possible.

Second, well before you leave your current employer, land at least one engaging and reasonably well-compensated part-time consulting stint around which a collection of assignments can be assembled. In fact, the employer from whom you are departing amicably could become your first client. Separating on favorable terms is conducive to your being retained on project assignments. Who else knows the business setting better than those who successfully operated in it for years? Who else is more fit to guarantee a running start on an important subject without the necessity for much orientation?

Proceeding in this way while you look for a permanent new post allows you to buy time. Working for one or more employers and/ or partaking of the gig economy will keep you active and help pay for continuing personal expenses. Meanwhile, you free yourself up to remain top of mind with the movers, shakers, and connectors to whom you have access.

I have admired those who can piece together part-time assignments to keep productive, while leaving ample room for the research, the networking, and the identification of a next full-time position.

While not for everyone, freeing yourself from the tedium of a full-time commitment can be liberating. Convincing others to retain you part-time is good practice for winning that desired more permanent spot. Writing your future on a blank sheet of paper is terrifying for some but clarifying for others.

Into which category do you fall?

Another option is to combine the two ideas. Stay in your current position and build on it. Declare for yourself another version of the end of either-or. Avoid the dangers of giving up full-time employment and take advantage of diversifying your working life.

This course of action is not easy. But it sure beats falling into the funk described by Henry Thoreau, who observed that most men and women live lives of quiet desperation. And it explains why career counselors urge not leaving where you are now situated professionally until you know your next destination.

There is no bad time to pursue a contact in search of the best professional landing place.

No season of the year, no hour of the day should be out of bounds.

Summer and winter are terrific because the pace of business is somewhat slower in those seasons. Presumably, important figures are then easier to reach and freer to help.

Spring and fall work well, because if you need something done, ask those who are really busy and fully staffed. Able executive assistants can help make things happen on behalf of a willing boss.

Place that vital phone call any time of the year between 6 and 8 a.m. or 6 and 7:30 p.m., because whoever you really wish to reach may well answer in the off-hours when their staff have either not yet reported to work or have already departed the premises. You will be pleasantly surprised by how many leaders and decision makers are often the first to arrive or the last to leave. Those same compulsive personalities often cannot resist picking up a ringing telephone or responding right away to an incoming email or text message.

Truth to tell, I cannot prove empirically that any of these assertions are valid. What matters is that I believe them to be true based on real-life experience. A positive attitude transforms itself into a self-fulfilling prophecy, while a pessimistic temperament leads to frustration, inaction, and depression. Winston Churchill put it well:

"A pessimist sees the difficulty in every opportunity; an optimist sees the opportunity in every difficulty."[4]

Being upbeat, treating each hour of every day as an occasion to present yourself and to ask for help is essential to success. Those you wish to influence, or from whom you seek help, will be drawn to your optimism and energy.

## Stuff Happens: The Involuntary Layoff

I did not see it coming.

I was taken by complete surprise.

Nine months earlier, in the fall of 1974, I had submitted my resignation from a terrific post as director of external affairs and special assistant to the executive director of the Jewish Board of Guardians (JBG), the nation's largest and most comprehensive mental health agency.

I had been at JBG for less than two years. I felt extremely fortunate to have worked so closely with the CEO, Jay Goldsmith, from whom I learned much about leadership, not least of the board of directors, and management, not least of a complex set of services and of gifted professionals. When I told Jay that I really needed to leave the agency, he asked a few questions to assure himself that I was not being utterly foolish. He expressed his doubts. My future at JBG was very bright. He asked me to think about what opportunities I would be leaving behind. He warned me about acting impulsively. But realizing that I was determined to take a chance, Jay wished me well. He offered his blessing.

I was departing to join the Aspen Institute. There, I would collaborate with my new boss, Waldemar A. Nielsen, noted author of *The Big Foundations*, among other books, former president of the African American Institute, and program officer at the Ford Foundation.

Wally had been in the audience for several speeches that I wrote and delivered. The subject was the then little-known nonprofit sector, writ large: its size, significance, challenges, and future agenda. Apparently, Wally liked what he had heard.

Concurrently, John Filer, the CEO of Aetna Life Insurance Company, was very upset. He had been asked by the Rockefeller family to chair a distinguished group of Americans who would serve on a special Commission on Private Philanthropy and Public Need. Millions of dollars had been spent on comprehensive research, dozens of meetings, and hundreds of consultations around the nation. Experts in particular fields of interest and in many specialties, like accounting and tax law, had been retained. The overall objective was to craft an unprecedented major report on the scope, impact, and promise of America's nonprofit sector. It was expected to advance recommendations on how nonprofits and the private foundations that supported them could be strengthened. The report was to be delivered to President Gerald Ford.

A draft had been circulated to a couple of dozen corporate, philanthropic, nonprofit, and governmental leaders. It was judged by almost all to be something of a dud. Dutiful, but dry and lacking in energetic ideas for invigorating this realm of American life. Particularly critical were the operating nonprofits. They felt strongly that too much attention had been paid to manipulating tax law on behalf of wealthy Americans. The commission was accused of being out of touch with the realities of nonprofit operations. They were referred to as grantees, recipients of foundation and individual support. As such, nonprofits seemed to be cast as passive beneficiaries of private largesse.

Quite unhappy with the negative reception accorded this draft, Filer turned to Nielsen. Would he be willing to examine the draft report and the voluminous studies and working papers that informed it? Would he then prepare a paper that better reflected what we now call the Third Sector, its performance as a contributor to American ideals and to our nation's competitive standing in the world?

Wally then reached me. He asked whether I would join him in New York City and then Aspen to develop the requested paper on an intense six-month timetable. Leaving JBG would not be easy for me, he recognized, so in addition to the Filer Commission assignment, how about my continuing to collaborate with him to co-author the definitive written work on this little understood, but influential, sphere of American life? "Reynold, the funds are secured for a solid two years of research, writing, and convening of experts. I know you agree with me that a first-rate book covering this vast and underappreciated field of activity is badly needed. Will you be my collaborator?"

Excited by the subject matter, delighted by the invitation, impressed by Wally's intellectual curiosity and the range of his interests, eager to meet members of the Filer Commission and other distinguished figures from around the country, I bade goodbye to Jay and to work on mental health and cast my lot with Wally.

We got along famously. Our jointly written white paper was very well received. Its themes and recommendations helped to shape the thoroughly revised final report. In addition, my participation in commission deliberations and in other groups convened by Wally was warmly recognized and appreciated.

At summer's end, Wally suggested that I return to New York City and begin familiarizing myself with extensive files at his office, 717 Fifth Avenue. Maybe I could even sketch out a book outline over the succeeding three weeks. I spent sixteen-hour days and weekends on this assignment and crafted a book prospectus that I thought held promise of launching me and Wally into a new phase of our work together.

When Wally returned to Manhattan and his office, he asked to have some words with me.

Actually, there were only three that mattered.

*You are fired.*

There had been no warning whatsoever. No red or even blinking yellow lights about our work or our relationship. Until that very moment, it was all thumbs-up and high fives.

I was dumbfounded. Blindsided. Furious. Deeply embarrassed.

Totally unfamiliar with how to conduct myself under such circumstances, I did everything wrong. I was twenty-nine years old and frightfully lacking in experience about how to protect myself and my family.

I did not attempt to engage in a conversation about the whys or wherefores of this surprising decision, let alone its timing. All Wally would say was that he had harbored second thoughts about having any coauthor, as all of his books until then were written only by him.

Why the 180-degree change of mind?

I didn't ask. He didn't tell.

Nor did I request any kind of transitional assistance. Might I stay with Aspen at the New York City office for three months or so, while looking high and low for a substitute position? Could Wally see his way to a severance of any kind to cushion this blow? Did he know of any open positions at the Aspen Institute or otherwise for which I might be qualified? Might he introduce me to some VIPs for prospecting interviews?

I put none of these questions to him.

It was September 1975. New York City was in a deep recession. Municipal bankruptcy loomed. Mayor Beame appeared entirely incompetent and unable to run the nation's largest city. The credibility of public officials could not have been lower. Good jobs were scarce: public, private, nonprofit. Wally must have known that he was delivering this news to me in a terrible economic environment. He also must have known that I had no reason to expect to be shown the door.

I was livid. My shattered ego and anger got the better of me. Upon hearing the news from Wally, I gathered my personal belongings, walked through that door he had opened, and never returned. Nor could I bring myself to ask to see Jay and report that his fears for my future had proven correct. I was now out on the street, so to say. Might JBG have anything for me? I could not swallow my pride and put the question to the very mentor who had befriended me. I didn't call the well-connected professional Jay Goldsmith, who knew me best and who could, and would, if asked, help me the most.

So, before I use myself as a case example of what to do in something of an emergency, when you need a job and have not prepared at all to look for one, here, from personal experience, is an encapsulation of what not to do.

Do not leave your employer in a huff. Do not fail to discuss the terms of separation. Particularly when you are being dismissed without notice and arbitrarily, ask for time and/or money to ease the transition. Such a request is not unexpected. And the funds that I should have requested were readily available to Wally. His budget could easily accommodate it.

Calm down and chill out. Do not react immediately when your emotions have taken over. Request time to meet with your soon-to-be former boss after you have composed yourself and recovered somewhat from the suddenness of devastating news.

And, most importantly, do not ever accept a job without engaging in due diligence about your employer. Yes, I had read all of Wally's books and many of his essays and speeches. But I never spoke with anyone who had ever worked with him, or for him. I never asked what it was really like to be his colleague. Especially in a work setting of just me, Wally, and an assistant, how could I possibly agree to a professional engagement without the functional equivalent of at least dating? At the very least, I could have suggested a luncheon conversation or two to acquire a better sense of what he was really like.

Now, if you unexpectedly lose a job, beyond what *not* to do, here is the six-point recovery plan I then hastily improvised. You may find it of some value.

**1. Keep busy. Take any part-time job you can. Staying active is important, psychologically and practically.**

For me, that meant teaching political science as an adjunct assistant professor at Herbert Lehman College-CUNY, resuming some part-time work in the teenage department of the Shorefront Y, and engaging in some paid public speaking gigs. Build on any such schedule of activity.

## 2. Ask for help. Hustle. Overcome your sense of disappointment.

Precisely because when you need a job it is hardly the ideal time to find one and precisely because a catastrophic local economy does not help, place your foot on the accelerator.

I reached anyone and everyone who might help. Former professors at Columbia Law School and the University of Virginia. Contacts within the Federation of Jewish Philanthropies, of which JBG was only one of many members. Conversations with a few associates of my parents. Even my long-term pediatrician, internist, and dentist were included on a growing phone list.

Having spent seven solid years in academia after college, there had been little time for me to build a support group. But I did whatever I could to connect with whoever I knew or even knew of.

Often, it is acquaintances drawn to you who are willing to help the most. Do not hesitate to reach them.

## 3. Leave home.

Jobs are hiding in the rough and tumble of the marketplace. Get out there and find them. Attend conferences, professional meetings, and networking breakfasts. Meet with anyone who can offer useful leads. Mix and mingle. Hand out business cards so those with whom you speak know how best to reach you.

## 4. Look forward.

It will be tempting to dwell on what just happened to you and why. Don't. As a workplace refugee, concentrate undistractedly on your resettlement, not on your resentment.

## 5. Volunteer.

Others around you in New York City need assistance. You have some income-producing gigs. You have set aside some money for that rainy day. Your spouse or companion may be working full- or part-time.

Sure, you are now in a fix. But there is no need to panic. Gain some satisfaction from helping others. Simultaneously, you may meet champions of the same cause who can assist you. It's all part of an effort to circulate and to make yourself better known. Besides, helping others far less fortunate will be good for your own morale.

## 6. Stay positive.

Summon the energy to believe in yourself. You misjudged the situation. You took a risk. It only paid off, partially. Get over the dismissal. Keep moving. Channel your anger into proving that there is a productive and satisfying working life ahead.

As predictions go, this last one proved to me to be on the money.

Seven months after my humiliating experience in Wally's company, I was appointed the executive director of the task force on the New York City fiscal crisis.

It was a new beginning, and my career never subsequently experienced so much as a hiccup.

Forty-five years have passed, and this failure still stings. It demonstrates that you can learn as much from committing an error in judgment as you can from multiple successes. Never again would I fail to think about what could go wrong in my current job and prepare for undesirable possibilities. Never again would I enter a new employment setting without learning as much as possible about it, my new boss, and my immediate colleagues.

Should the unanticipated happen to you, I hope this encapsulation of my early career debacle will serve both as an instructive negative model and as a positive comeback story.

## Societal Influences and Trends

Many employers today have trouble finding and keeping qualified employees for key openings at all levels in the organization. They are responding by paying more attention to entry-level salaries, offering more job training, and developing clearer paths for advancement.

The increased availability of universal pre-K for kids at four years of age holds the promise of preparing them for basic literacy, numeracy, and social skills, even as it offers working parents relief from childcare expenses and peace of mind about the health and safety of their kids.

States and cities throughout the nation are enacting increases in the minimum wage, adequate periods of parental and sick leave, more predictable work schedules, and subsidies for mass transportation. The fears that such mandated improvements in the terms and conditions of employment would lead to fewer jobs and more layoffs have gone largely unrealized.

Colleges and universities are responding to the crisis of student debt and under- or delayed employment of their graduates. Philanthropists like David Geffen for the University of California and Ken Langone for New York University are taking the lead on fully subsidizing tuitions of all medical school students, and Mayor Bloomberg has announced doing so for every undergraduate at Johns Hopkins University. Most recently, the private equity billionaire Robert F. Smith announced in his commencement address to the Morehouse College class of 2019 that he would contribute enough funds to pay off all of the loans of those graduating, a total sum of $40 million.

They are hardly alone. There is widespread awareness that very smart poor and working-class kids fully able to succeed at private colleges and public universities do not even bother to apply. They simply do not have anywhere near the funds to pay for tuition and room and board.

In the last decade, according to David Leonhardt of the *New York Times*, states have cut college funding by an average of 16 percent per student.[5] Financial barriers are simply too high for most students from working-class families to vault. It is now dawning on elected and appointed officials that public universities subject to such budget cuts are being compelled to raise tuition to unaffordable levels.

Lowering these barriers to entry through legislation and through the adjustment of institutional priorities is underway. For example, in New York State, public college and university tuition is now free of charge to any student from a family of four earning under $150,000 annually who maintains acceptable grades. In colleges and universities around the nation, presidents and boards of directors are placing much higher on their priorities raising funds to offer substantial scholarship assistance to those in need. Declared candidates for president like Elizabeth Warren and Bernie Sanders have highlighted both college debt elimination plans and free tuition at public universities. The spirit of progressive reform is in the air.

Employers recognize the desirability of investing much more in their workforce. Starbucks, Costco, Deloitte, Amazon, American Express, Wegmans, McKinsey, and Accenture[6] are among the hundreds of firms announcing in recent years the offer of more tuition assistance, the expansion of their in-house "universities," the provision of free access to high-quality online course offerings, the spending of additional funds on in-house training programs, the enlargement of apprentice and mentoring initiatives, and increased numbers of flexible workdays.

Leading law firms have long focused on the competition for talent. Their terms and conditions of employment reflect the fierce determination to attract and retain the most gifted lawyers and support staff. Choosing between the top forty firms that offer the most generous benefits and alluring working environments is not easy. But Cravath, Swaine, and Moore; Wachtell Lipton; Cahill

Gordon; Paul, Weiss & Rifkind; and Boies Schiller surely number in that company.

Meanwhile, schools increasingly recognize that counseling services are not luxuries but essential to the welfare of their students. Hiring able and experienced staff to direct school-to-career mobility is indispensable. Those charged with this responsibility must have experience in government, business, or the nonprofit sectors. They must be able to organize alumni to offer students internships, gap-year assignments, mentoring, and part-time jobs. Adding to the faculty adjunct professors and practitioners in residence who know where exciting job opportunities are likely to surface and how best to pursue them is a growing trend worth watching. These personnel who are closer to the employment marketplace must work for CEOs who view the exposure of students to workplace opportunities throughout the year, but most importantly during vital summer months, as a matter of importance.

These are all vibrant and encouraging signs. As you consider which business and nonprofit job openings are worth competing to fill, remember those firms on the forefront of valuing their high-potential employees. Such initiatives are useful indicators of potential good places to work. The responsibility is yours to locate opportunity and to mobilize friends and colleagues and their networks to help seize it. Be alert to the existence of new and enhanced employee benefits and what they might portend for you.

But be careful. It is also easy to be distracted by external developments and supposed trends, some of which are alarmist or just plain irrelevant.

In the latter category, consider reports of the national, regional, or local unemployment rate, or whether a recession is looming, or the direction the stock market may be taking. These news items and the commentary they generate are hard to ignore. Often, they are upsetting, and they can set you off course.

The question you need to keep asking is whether any of these macro developments should influence your personal job hunt. After all, you are only looking for *one* promising position.

In the former category comes the work of prognosticators and futurists.

Now you will hear a lot about how artificial intelligence, self-driving cars, automation, big data analytics, machine learning, virtual reality, and robots will put millions of Americans out of work. Perhaps so. Count me dubious.

Remember that the ATM was bound to radically reduce the number of bank tellers and offices around the country. Remember that the advent of e-books would cause the very end of the independent bookstore. Remember that streaming services would severely reduce the number of movie theaters and the attractiveness of live entertainment. Remember that television would abolish radio and that handheld devices and desktop computers would eliminate television. None of these predictions have come true.

To the contrary, JPMorgan announced in 2019 its intention to open four hundred additional branches nationwide in the next few years.[7] It is hardly alone. Independent bookstores, after diminishing in number with the advent of the e-book, have now resumed a significant growth spurt. Between 2009 and 2015, the number of independent bookstores expanded by 35 percent, from 1,651 to 2,470.[8] Movie ticket sales and revenue are in very healthy shape, as are the comparable numbers for Broadway.[9] As to audio and radio, unit sales of audiobooks are zooming,[10] and the sheer number of podcasts is growing phenomenally.

Only the passage of time will tell whether the latest prognostications of gloom and doom for the job market due to technological advances are more right than wrong and over how many decades. In the meantime, such speculation will not bring you any closer to that meaningful job. These technological developments and their implications are all important and intriguing. But how relevant are they to the search that preoccupies you today?

Focus on your task with intensity. Do not allow yourself to become bewildered by external events, let alone depressed by them. Remember, the general economic and business news of the day may be dreadful, but how does that possibility really affect your job prospects? Remember, futurists have often been wrong and, in any event, you are not looking for work a decade or more from today. You are seeking exciting employment now.

## The Job Seeker as Athlete

If you are in the mood to role-play as you search for work, once again, think tennis.

Before every swing, championship players prepare their footwork as they approach the ball, moving their body toward where it is likely to land. They train incessantly. They control their eating habits carefully. They sleep soundly. They assess their opponents' strengths and weaknesses and arrive at the stadium with a game plan.

Before ever walking onto the center court, championship athletes abide by strict discipline in training, conditioning, nutrition, and mental alertness. Ideally, they come to the competition physically and psychologically fit.

When a tennis player appears in a major match, he or she is alone on the court. There are no time-outs. There is no halftime. No opportunity exists to consult with a coach or to receive advice about a specific play or a change in game strategy. Unlike football, where both can be communicated to the quarterback through his headset or at halftime and, unlike basketball, where the coach's time-out can be an important element of a game-winning strategy, the tennis player is alone. Any help emanating from the sidelines is strictly prohibited. Thinking through tactics and managing the tension and pressure of the game comes without guidance. Even the professional boxer has a manager in his corner, whispering in his ear after each round. Not so in tennis. There is a great deal of value to be extracted by spending part of your time pretending to be participating in a sport that places a premium on self-reliance.

Ultimately, though, the job seeker is much more like the football and basketball player or the prizefighter, rather than the tennis buff. Coaches, mentors, and advisers are all available to you. In conducting research about job openings. In learning with whom you would work most closely if selected for a job. In acquiring detailed guidance about the interview process. All of these steps on the road to meaningful work need not be so foreign or mysterious. Assemble a team to support you. You need not be on your own.

If 80 percent of life is just showing up in the right place at the appointed hour, the other 20 percent is energetically arriving well prepared, well composed, and suitably attired. Your encounters with the decision maker are critical to success.

You should aim to have the impact of your presence before a potential employer just as strong and favorable as it can be. Winning that coveted job is itself very hard work. It is not a hobby.

Start now and do not stop until you can genuinely declare mission accomplished. And then gear up for succeeding at your new post, without blinding yourself to next career steps.

Champagne is waiting on ice for you and all those who have come to your side.

Congratulations.

But toast not to the valuable job you just received, but to a future in and beyond it, one filled with promise. That which lies ahead might best be put in the form of a universal question.

What is it that really makes life worth living?

# -9-

# The Quest for Meaning

---

*"Success, like happiness, cannot be pursued; it must ensue, and it only does so as the unintended side effect of one's dedication to a cause greater than oneself or as the by-product of one's surrender to a person other than oneself."*

—Victor E. Frankel[1]

*"I rise every morning torn between a desire to help save the world and a desire to savor the world. It makes it hard to plan my day."*

—E. B. White[2]

*"There is no life that couldn't be immortal, if only for a moment."*

—Wisława Szymborska[3]

To find your satisfying place in life is a process that, if you are fortunate, never ends. Identifying what is most meaningful to you can remain constant, like devotion to family. Even then, the forms that commitment may assume will change over time. And so may the number of additional goals you decide to pursue.

Parent as caregiver. Parent as financial provider. Parent as friend and counselor. Parent as teacher. Parent as standard setter. Parent as reliable source of empathic listening and of learned advice.

For most of us, an enduring commitment to a life partner, to children, to parents, to siblings, and to the extended members of a family is imperative. For many, family solidarity, while utterly necessary, is not sufficient to experience a fully realized life on earth. If dedication to family encompassed all of your attention, life would seem somewhat empty, or at the very least, incomplete.

Sigmund Freud posited that only two activities truly matter to human beings: love and work. Beyond family, many draw satisfaction from professional success and its associated financial benefits. The corporate executive. The consummate lawyer. The skilled accountant. The assembly line worker. They all can experience pride in the quality of their work. Some even benefit from significant promotion: to senior vice president, to senior partner, to managing director, or to floor supervisor.

Electricians, farmers, plumbers, carpenters, construction workers—they too highly prize excellent performance and draw much pride from their tangible accomplishments. Finding higher purpose in work is not confined to those clothed in a white collar or who spend the bulk of their days behind a desk and in front of a keyboard.

## The What and the How

You can be part of a mission-driven, purposeful organization that performs good deeds. It can enjoy an excellent reputation. And you can still be miserable in that workplace.

Conversely, your role in an organization can be to contribute to the profit of partners and associates or added value for shareowners. Only incidental social benefits could be attached to your labors. Even in this incarnation, you can, with Jeff Bezos, be so happy that you claim to tap-dance to work each morning.

Leaving aside the purpose of the employer you choose to join, there are well-established norms for what can render the experience gratifying.

Can you actually witness the results of your and your team's efforts?

Does the employer offer you a measure of freedom and control over when and where business is conducted?

Is your environment nurturing? Does it provide opportunities for continuous learning, for training, and for mentoring?

Employees appreciate a range of discretion and a semblance of influence over the circumstances of their working environment. They relish being recognized and rewarded for their achievements. They welcome opportunities for refining their skills and replenishing their intellectual capital. They are thrilled when their employer does not care about much more than the quality of their work product and its timely delivery. Whether you are in the office or thousands of miles away matters hardly at all to a beloved boss.

Meaningful, then, is not just a descriptor for *what* you choose to do, the content of your work, but also for the way in which you are encouraged to do it, the *how* of your labor.

Perhaps that is why more than 50 percent of American workers are unhappy at work. They are dissatisfied with their pay, working conditions, and prospects for the future.[4] They feel their talents and skills are underutilized. Their employers are failing to recognize the significant gap between what the organization needs and what its workers can contribute to satisfy them. This low level of job satisfaction is widespread across all age ranges and at all levels of most firms.

## Life's Motivations

Refining your skills and continuously improving your performance at work can be immensely satisfying. It can entail more than personal pride and economic benefit. It can also encompass the creation of new jobs, increased returns to shareowners, flourishing clients, and enhanced efficiency. These are accomplishments that extend over and above self. They contribute immensely to social welfare.

Developing new products and services, or enhancing them, can increase our nation's economic productivity. Continuously improving how they are designed, manufactured, and delivered is a source of fulfillment. America's innovative economy creates many jobs offering these tangible results. All those responsible for them should feel a justifiable sense of pride.

Remember when it was fashionable in some quarters to be very disturbed about what was then called "the digital divide"? The concern was that only the wealthy and the middle class could afford to secure easy access to handheld computer power and connectivity unprecedented in its reach. Today, appliances like smart phones are almost ubiquitous. Their utility is way up. Their price, way down. The same can be observed about radios, televisions, clothing, airline fares, and entertainment, all available at costs the working class can afford to pay. To be involved in improving the lives of countless others, enabling them to acquire and experience what would have been entirely out of reach, well, it doesn't get much better than that.

When you combine these occupational outcomes with nurturing family relationships and private pleasures, like enjoyable hobbies, fulfilling lives materialize.

In our capitalist society, there are those who measure success differently. They calculate their net worth. Is it growing rapidly enough? Do I have available funds adequate to satisfy acquisitive habits, the art or wine collection, the third or fourth home, flying first-class or by private jet, the yacht, admission to the most exclusive private clubs and gated communities? For a growing segment of deca- and centi-millionaires and billionaires, these are among the things that matter most.

Are you faring as well financially as your social and professional peers? That is the question that drives many in life. That is how much of the one percent at the top of the world's economic ladder keep score.

It is often said that for such capitalists, "he who dies with the most toys, wins."

Wins what, I often wonder. Isn't the accumulation of wealth a means to an end, rather than an end in itself? Isn't it possible that the capitalist, driven by measures of accumulated wealth, finds that what had been the means threatens to devour life's ends? Family solidarity. Social welfare. Help to the less fortunate. Personal contentment. A legacy of which you can be proud.

By contrast, consider Andrew Carnegie's simply stated words of wisdom: "He who dies rich, dies disgraced."

Or ponder the question of Julius Rosenwald, the founder of Sears and Roebuck and noted philanthropist. A century ago, he asked:

> Shall we devote the few precious days of our existence only to buying and selling, only to comparing sales of the same day the year before… and when the end comes to leave as little a taxable estate as possible as the final triumph and achievement of our lives?
>
> Surely there is something finer and better in life, something that dignifies it with at least some little touch of the divine.[5]

While driven by a consuming fixation on stock prices and options and on earnings per share, still there are undeniable indirect societal benefits that accrue from this exercise in capitalism. Even as the rich may focus on the status wealth confers and the possessions it can command, the lives of fellow citizens can also be improved.

Here is none other than Adam Smith on the subject:

> Every individual endeavors to employ his capital so that what it produces may be of greatest value… He intends only his own security, only his own gain… By pursuing his interest he frequently promotes that of society more effectively than when he really intends to promote it.[6]

Adam Smith notwithstanding, the ethos that when it comes to capitalism nothing succeeds like excess may, after a while, feel empty, even stultifying. The profit motive is often not enough to complete a life. These extrinsic motivations and rewards spark a desire in many adults for an intrinsic companion. A sense of self that contains more than material measures of personal success, one that encompasses a concern for the needs and aspirations of others, even strangers.

I am often asked whether you can combine earning a living with directly assisting needy people and noble causes.

Of course you can. Just follow the example of millions of your fellow citizens.

One road to fulfillment is lodged in the "helping professions." The social worker, the nurse, the teacher, the home care aid, the nanny, the physical therapist. Finding gratification in healing the sick, nurturing the toddler or the aging, moving the struggling student to mastery of subject matter and growing self-confidence. It is hard to imagine more gratifying work.

And what of the inner-city physician, the pastor, the uniformed officer, and the many varieties of first responder? From sickness to health, from depression to normalcy, and from life-threatening situations to safety, these are among the roles that millions of Americans find so satisfying.

Or think of still other millions of Americans in our armed forces, or engaged in humanitarian service abroad, or who dedicate their lives to the American Red Cross, or the International Rescue Committee, or the Salvation Army, or Habitat for Humanity, or Boys and Girls Clubs, or to their favorite arts or environmental organization.

The impact of these kinds of associations on individual lives is palpable and profound. It alone is reason enough to choose a life of service in a helping profession. The benefits to others of those who labor day in and day out in this kind of work also touch the lives of additional millions of Americans. They also offer time, talent, and treasure to mission-driven, nonprofit causes in their off hours.

Remarkably, a significant commitment to helping the less fortunate also rewards the caregiver, the volunteer, and the donor. That combination is powerful. Perhaps it helps explain why so many Americans who do not interact professionally with needy individuals or families choose to spend precious time away from work attending to the challenges of poverty and tackling other worthy causes.

We know that benevolent interventions in the formative years of children and in the lives of needy adults are critical to their well-being. We know how important caregivers are to our health and serenity. What we are learning is just how many benefits accrue to those who spend a significant chunk of their lives helping others.[7]

Serving as mentors, role models, tutors, soccer coaches, and English-as-a-second-language instructors is thoroughly pleasurable. Evidence mounts that involvement at critical moments in the lives of needy children and adults inures to the welfare of the volunteer. Surprising is how much connecting to other human beings and noble causes brings physical and mental health benefits to the donor.

When I raised hundreds of millions of dollars and recruited dozens of volunteers as the president of Lincoln Center, I was fond of offering to any benefactor of a consequential gift of funds, services, or expertise these five guarantees: You will sleep better. You will live longer. You will be happier. You shall enjoy an unobstructed pathway to heaven *and* find yourself ushered to aisle seats on arrival. Social scientists are discovering many a truth in this jest, at least when it comes to the first three of my proffered entitlements to be bestowed on the generous.[8]

Another method of securing the welfare of others springs from a desire to help on a large scale, not one on one, or face to face, but in reforming government service and changing public policy. Measurably improving the lives of large numbers of Americans and people worldwide is a powerful motivator. Examples include those inside and outside government who helped President Clinton enact and strengthen the earned income tax credit, an important source of funds to lift up those who work full-time at wages that would otherwise consign them to poverty. All who advocated for and helped realize President Bush's successful anti-HIV/AIDS initiative in Africa. Enabling more than twenty million medically indigent Americans to secure health insurance and eliminating penalties for preexisting conditions and lifetime caps on needed care in support of President Obama's landmark accomplishment, the passage of the Affordable Care Act.

These are but three of thousands of ways in which shaping public policy and how it is implemented can change tens of millions of lives for the better. You can participate as a member of the legislative, executive, or judicial branches at the local, state, or federal level. You can join others in advocating for change with these very officials. Citizen movements will welcome your involvement. You can be employed by, or assist with time and financial resources, any of the hundreds of thousands of nonprofits implementing needed programs.

If the helping professions are pathways to providing assistance one client at a time, public policy practitioners are force multipliers. Governmental reform often takes longer to realize success, but the numbers who benefit are potentially huge.

These approaches are not mutually exclusive. Those working with individuals or small groups of disadvantaged are sometimes moved to join advocates in seeking important public policy change.

And those initially drawn to government service striving for wholesale change report on how satisfying are the retail accomplishments of helping individual citizens along the way. Speeding the acquisition of Social Security benefits or of a green card. Overcoming bureaucracy to help enroll a citizen in Medicaid or assist a veteran in admission to a VA hospital. Coming to the rescue of an innocent law-abiding taxpayer caught up in a seemingly impenetrable web of IRS inquiries.

It is so fulfilling to witness the relief and gratitude of those whose lives were improved because of successful casework. It is at least equally moving to know that legislative or regulatory reform prevented harm to nameless millions or remedied injustice to large numbers of Americans or foreigners.

In sum, there are many varieties of meaningful work. And even more for a worthwhile life, one that combines what is pursued at the workplace with what can be accomplished civically and philanthropically.

The founder of eBay, Pierre Omidyar, has created an innovative business model of social change that combines commercial, nonprofit, and governmental entities. He claims that the larger the scale of the problem to be addressed, the greater the necessity for all three sectors working together.

> ...[you] really can make the world better in any sector, in nonprofits, in business, or in government. It's not a question of one sector struggling against another or "giving back" versus "taking away." That's old thinking. A true philanthropist will use every tool he can to make an impact.[9]

Public activism and nonprofit leadership are available as full-time or supplemental endeavors.

Family. Country. Humanity.

It is hard to imagine a completely rewarding life that does not address this hallowed trinity of high purpose in some significant manner. That is why I am so encouraged by the quest for meaning in younger generations of Americans. They are conspicuous by their presence in advocating to combat climate change, to decrease opportunity gaps, to advocate for universal health care, a much higher federal minimum wage, and sensible gun control. From the #MeToo movement to Black Lives Matter, from the Parkland high school student campaign to Occupy Wall Street. The record number of young people who voted in the 2018 "off-year" congressional election was gratifying to witness. It appears that concern for worldly personal success and worries about managing student debt have not deterred growing numbers of gen X-ers and millennials from engaging in social and political reform movements of many kinds.

Of course, the motivation for many to contribute to the welfare of others is religious or spiritual in origin.

I was raised to favor the underdog, the downtrodden, the disadvantaged. I was taught to focus on the needy stranger in my midst, to believe in the Talmud's teaching that:

> It is not required of thee to complete the task, but neither art thou free to desist therefrom… He who saves one life, it is as if he has saved the world.

Others are motivated by the golden rule. "Do unto others as you would have them do unto you," or that "no man is an island unto himself." It is the gospel that commands us to receive the stranger and to relieve his wants.

In the words of Jesus himself comes this injunction: "Unto whomsoever much is given, of him shall much be required, and to whom men have committed much, of him they will ask for more."

Whatever the source of your belief, secular or religious, Frankel's words that open this chapter are filled with wisdom. Surrender to a cause beyond self and to a person other than self and genuine happiness will be yours to enjoy.

# – 10 –

# Beyond Self

---

*"Porridge is helpful and having a job you enjoy."*
—Alfred Smith, the *New York Times*,
March 31, 2019, when asked how he ex-
plains his longevity at the age of 111

*"A sound process to formulate and execute foreign policy does not
guarantee success, but a defective one all but insures failure."*
—Winston Lord, *Kissinger on Kissinger*[1]

Foreign policy is not the only subject about which it can be claimed that a sound process is a necessary but not sufficient condition for success.

That which is true abroad has as much validity closer to home.

So, what is your process for determining the next jobs you desire and how will you go about securing one of them?

Are there coaches, mentors, and advisers on whom you can rely?

Developing an informal set of career counselors is always help-ful in the lifelong process of shaping a career. Draw them from friends, current and former colleagues, clients, and partners. Their environmental scans and their knowledge of your strengths and your potential are invaluable.

The number of nurturing models varies widely.

## All in the Family (Almost)

It is Sunday evening at 10 p.m. Eastern time. Any and every Sunday evening, fifty-two weeks a year, on a conference call are the Medoff children, all six of them: Kara, Ari, Sar, Carmi, Gena, and Mica. These siblings convene weekly without fail to converse and to compare notes about their lives.

Challenges at work and at home. Developments in society and politics. Plans for travel. Advice about dining and arts and culture. Reaching decisions about how to invest funds that each member of the family has decided to contribute to a common pool and how to allocate funds jointly set aside for charitable contributions.

What films to see. Whom to be sure to meet. The best books to read. Shows and exhibits that just shouldn't be missed. And, of course, assistance in thinking through the next steps up the ladder at work or across the catwalk to another position at a new place of employment.

Ari, after graduating from Duke, received an MBA and master's in public policy from Harvard Business School and the Harvard Kennedy School of Government. Then he founded what has become the largest home healthcare service in all of North Carolina. Nurse Care of North Carolina is now operating under the name AROSA, having already expanded to five additional states.

Kara, a graduate of Duke who also earned an MBA from Harvard, began her career as a Broadway producer, winning a Tony Award for a production of *Long Day's Journey into Night* when she was twenty-four years old. She later worked at Lincoln Center as director of strategic planning and as the managing director of a successful international consulting firm lodged in the world's most prominent performing arts center. Her latest professional incarnation is as the executive director of American Ballet Theatre.

Sar Medoff graduated from Princeton and received a master's degree in public policy from Harvard's Kennedy School of Government. He then studied at the Icahn School of Medicine at Mount Sinai. After receiving his MD degree, he became a resident at

Emory Healthcare and an attending physician in emergency medicine at Vituity. Throughout his career, time has been found to take regular trips to Ethiopia, offering medical care to those in need.

Mica Medoff graduated with a degree in art history at Colgate. She worked for the art dealer Larry Gagosian and for a leading public relations firm. Her latest position is as a manager of external affairs at the International Rescue Committee, applying her experience to a mission she cares about deeply.

Carmi is a Duke graduate who has been employed as a research coordinator at Disney|ABC Television Group and then at a fintech start-up before enrolling in Harvard Business School.

And Gena, the youngest of these remarkable siblings, graduated from Franklin & Marshall and is pursuing a joint degree in social work and international policy at the University of Denver. During her studies, she has worked on organic farms in New Zealand, Florida, and South Carolina and was drawn to Kenya as well to assist on several agricultural projects.

From these extraordinarily diverse work experiences, educational backgrounds, geographic locations, and family configurations arise rich sources of advice and guidance. Ranging in age from twenty-five to forty, what the Medoff siblings enjoy is nothing less than a homemade cabinet of counselors where love and trust in one another combine to form a common bond.

To be part of an extended family of such accomplishment and of such commitment is a blessing. Every Sunday night is supplemented, of course, with plenty of one-on-one conversations in between. The Medoffs lean on each other not as exclusive repositories of advice, but as excellent points of departure for expanding their networks and extending their reach. Add personal discipline, ambition, and intellectual curiosity. That blend is a potent formula for success and for offering help to others less fortunate.

More power to them.

Few of us are situated by age, by upbringing, and by proclivity to turn to family members for leads to meaningful work and consequential lives. Certainly not with the sophistication, continuity, intimacy, and dedication of the Medoff family.

Not to worry. Supplement whatever reliable advice you do receive from parents and brothers and sisters by meeting helpful advisers from your alumni chapter, professional associations, peers, and mentors at work, at public events, and in volunteer activities. Befriending those with whom you enjoy common interests and aspirations should be part and parcel of your weekly routine. Parents of children in the same school, or on the same athletic team, can also find themselves linking up in ways useful to their career advancement.

What's important is to think of these associations not as isolated, compartmentalized parts of your life, but as integrated into a constant search for meaningful work and for an honorable life.

Closely observe how others conduct themselves at your workplace and in your extracurricular activities. Those to whom you are drawn because of their knowledge, social and professional networks, and approachability are likely candidates to become informal advisers, information sources, even mentors.

It would be splendid if you could find or organize a "kitchen cabinet" to guide you through life's personal and professional transitions. It would be lovely to have available a personal board of directors to consult with, on call. For virtually all of us, however, it is we who must be the convener, the organizer of counselors responsive to requests for guidance. Compiling notes on who offered what advice, recommended what to read, and provided leads on others to interview falls to each of us. So does a continuing assessment of the value of these encounters with people and ideas.

## Persistence

If the Medoff family is situated at one end of the collaborative continuum, my assistant of four years, Henry Wainhouse, can be found at the other. He flies solo. Well, almost.

After graduating from the University of Vermont, Henry taught elementary school kids for two years in the Bronx and then sixth graders for two years at a charter school in Brooklyn. Many of these youngsters were growing up in poverty and came from unstable homes. By all accounts, Henry was a superb teacher, admired by colleagues and befriended by his students. The work was tough. The pay middling. The expectations high, most of them set by Henry himself.

When I met Henry, he had decided to leave teaching and to enroll in law school. While working for me full-time, Henry studied conscientiously, nay, relentlessly and obsessively for his Law School Admission Test. Raised in modest economic circumstances, Henry was prepared to assume the substantial debt burdens necessitated by tuition, room, and board, but only if he could enroll in either Harvard or Columbia Law School. Having matriculated at Columbia Law myself, I knew how formidable were the obstacles to admission.

But Henry seemed bound and determined. He aimed for the best legal education. He hoped for enrollment in schools that would help him compete for desirable law firm positions and judicial clerkships. I was worried about Henry setting his sights too high and gently suggested broadening the pool of schools to which he might apply. He wouldn't hear of it.

Well, Henry fell somewhat shy of the LSAT grades needed and was turned down, not only by Harvard and Columbia, but also by Fordham Law, to which he had grudgingly applied as somewhat of a safety school, probably as a concession to me!

Honestly, I am not sure who was more heartbroken by these rejections. I have rarely encountered as smart, as intellectually curious, as well disciplined, and as thoughtful a young man. Possessed of excellent writing and presentation skills and able to think quickly on his feet, Henry would become a very fine lawyer. I was sure of it. And I conveyed as much and more in glowing letters of recommendation.

All for naught. And, then, shockingly, rather than retake the LSAT and apply again to Harvard and Columbia, Henry decided to enroll in a decidedly less well-known and less highly rated institution, Brooklyn Law School. His new idea was to rank high enough in his first-year class to transfer to Columbia or NYU Law School. Frankly, the chance for success with this new strategy seemed slim to me, if only because there are very few open slots in the second year of excellent law schools.

Grit, determination, and sheer knock-down, drag-out hard work won the day. Henry did emerge at the very top of his first-year Brooklyn Law School class. With just a little help from references like me, he was admitted to Columbia on the strength of his first-year grades. His academic record at Columbia was also superlative. Henry, having completed his first year at the prestigious law firm of Jones Day, and having been admitted to the practice of law by the New York Bar Association, is now working as a clerk to Judge Lorna Schofield in the Southern District of New York.

There are lessons that all of us can take away from Henry's experience. Hard work matters. Self-confidence matters. Resilience matters. Networking is not the exclusive pathway to that meaningful job and rewarding life. There are many roads to Rome.

Henry remains hungry. For experience, for a measure of material success, and for addressing some of America's leading challenges.

This is a guy to keep your eye on.

With limited time to pursue the ideas that come your way, setting priorities is essential. Finding that first or next position is itself a real job. Do not underestimate the time it will take and the intellectual and emotional energy it will require.

And, under no circumstances, accept the maxim that you "learn in your twenties and earn in your thirties." Learning is a lifelong proposition. When you stop learning, you stop living. Period.

## A Life of the Mind

Purposeful reading can help inform your search not just for meaningful work, but for a deeply informed and enriching life. All of us are limited in the number of people we can meet, organizations we can encounter and the breadth of the network we can create and sustain. But exposure to personalities, ideas, and institutions in books and periodicals, podcasts and blogs, is powerfully broadening. Please do not gainsay how helpful the written and spoken word can be throughout your professional and personal journeys.

When my parents died, one soon after the other, I found myself disposing of their personal effects. They lived very modestly and were hardly collectors, hoarders, or otherwise acquisitive. Still, the accumulation of memorabilia, furniture, clothing, and phonograph records, among other material goods, overwhelmed me. I did not know what they had in mind for me to do with them. Reaching decisions about who in our small family would receive what and which objects should be discarded entirely was painfully difficult. The process exacted an emotional toll.

Through tears of mourning, I pledged not to leave that kind of inadvertent burden to my children. Gradually, then, my wife and I have been donating many valuables that others can use while we are alive. By far the most time-consuming task has been properly disposing of books, as our library contained some ten thousand volumes.

Giving most of them away, somewhat to my surprise, became a tender, affecting experience. These books had been my tutors, guides, and intellectual companions. They had informed so much of how I view the world and my place in it. For many, I could recall with precision where and when I devoured them and the impact that each had on my life. Necessarily, I was dismantling the building blocks of my mind, and with them, so many intellectual and personal associations that I had formed.

Whispering goodbye was not easy. I was losing pieces of myself. I felt depleted. I still do.

## Beyond Self: Service to Others

I am a lucky guy.

My travel through life has allowed me to arrive at many different destinations. Shaping public policy. Running summer camps for kids. Rejuvenating the 92nd Street Y and expanding its educational, social service, residential, recreational, and performing arts programming. Teaching undergraduate and graduate students. Consulting. Writing. Providing leadership to AT&T's very early exploration in breakthrough corporate social responsibility programs. Tithing our family's earnings to charitable giving.

Helping the International Rescue Committee through a dangerously vulnerable stage in its economic and organizational well-being. Assembling a large team of fellow employees and resourceful volunteers to overcome conflict and divisiveness, transforming the physical infrastructure, artistic facilities, and public spaces of the renowned Lincoln Center. Serving on several dozen nonprofit boards of directors, as a trustee of two formidable family foundations, and as lead director of one outstanding banking enterprise.

Looking back on a life filled with diverse opportunities, I think as much of those who have been personally helped as of major institutional accomplishments. I take as much pride in the mentees whom I advised and the teammates who worked together to accomplish noble ends as I do in the substantive results of our work. Many of my colleagues have moved on to very successful careers, filled with meaning.

Yes, due in no small measure to the task force on the New York City fiscal crisis, Mayor Beame's and Governor Carey's proposed draconian cuts to the health and social safety net protecting the poor did not happen. Yes, AT&T took a courageous and multifaceted stand against apartheid in South Africa and for combating HIV/AIDS very early, when few other firms were willing to enlist in these causes. Yes, hundreds of thousands of additional New Yorkers and tourists enjoy Lincoln Center. It now welcomes them with many new and inviting public spaces and with free, high-quality artistic programs. And, yes, the IRC's decision to airlift food into the remote areas of Kosovo, when no other government or NGO was prepared to do so, saved hundreds of lives, while its investment in internet provider services created thousands of livelihoods.

These and many other expansive accomplishments still feel good. Most endure. But what I remember as much are the students who remain inspired by what they can contribute to social enterprise and the young protégés and collaborators, some of whom have become major figures in the current generation of nonprofit leaders and philanthropists.[2] Out there on this planet of ours are myriad inequities, injustices, and suffering. By finding meaningful work or supplementing your day job with engagement in public service or nonprofit endeavors, you can invest more fully in worthy causes and worthwhile organizations.

Called for here is not grandiosity or superhuman accomplishment. The pleasure and thrill derived from "do[ing] what you can, with what you have, where you are,"[3] while it may be modest, can well be more than enough. That refugee family, that first-generation immigrant, that struggling student, and that suicidal veteran can flourish with your help. I invite you to "experience immortality, if only for a moment."

Believe, with Robert Kennedy, these words and do not hesitate to *Start Now*.

> It is from the numberless diverse acts of courage and belief that human history is shaped. Each time a man stands up for an ideal, or acts to improve the lot of others, or strikes out against injustice, he sends a tiny ripple of hope, and crossing each other from a million different centers of energy and daring, those ripples build a current which can sweep down the mightiest walls of oppression and resistance.[4]

Join those who engage in such acts of advancing human welfare with most of your working days, or in your off hours. You will experience a level of contentment that only meaningful work, combined with charitable and philanthropic activity, can fully furnish. For those who choose to leave their families, their country, and the less fortunate better than they found them, the porridge is waiting, and it is delicious.

# Not Done Yet

## Lives Unfinished

---

*"A society grows great when old men plant trees whose shade they know they will never sit in."*
—Lucy Larcom, "Plant a Tree"[1]

My good fortune has not been confined to holding full-time posts filled with challenge and meaning. Simultaneously, I was determined to engage in other gratifying and pleasurable pursuits. For some of them, I was paid. For others, I volunteered.

Testing myself in multiple professional and pro bono roles is a consistent life theme. My commercial and nonprofit clients could hardly care less about whether I can hold my own in teaching demanding students at Harvard Business School. The publishers of my books are singularly unimpressed with my service on nonprofit and foundation boards of directors. The trustees of the institutions I served as president were largely indifferent to my work as an author. Audiences assembled for my frequent public speaking engagements did not take notice of my role as consultant or as the lead director of First Republic Bank. Employees of the organizations I helped lead understandably focused on conditions in their full-time home, where they lived, professionally. As to the rest of my working life, shoulders shrugged.

For me, though, all of these incarnations were of a piece. They compelled me to exercise different intellectual and operational muscles. They fed an insatiable curiosity. They invited me to meet hundreds of fascinating people and to encounter scintillating ideas. These experiences informed my thinking and animated my life. Every pecuniary and charitable commitment contributed to the fund of knowledge and skill I could bring to my other assignments.

Students and deans. Readers and editors. Recruiters and bosses. Employees. Audience members. Clients. Fellow trustees. All subjected me to thorough inspection and appraisal. Each held me to a different standard of performance, appropriate to the particular situational setting and to my specific assignment.

The natural and understandable tendency for associates to focus exclusively on what you could do for their favorite cause or institution, setting aside whatever else preoccupied you, applied as well to my major investment in the nonprofit sector.

There are what I refer to as legacy concerns and activities. These are commitments to places and causes carried over from the years I had been devoted to them professionally.

The places? The 92nd Street Y. The International Rescue Committee. Lincoln Center. The Revson Foundation. American Ballet Theatre.

The causes? Relieving the plight of the poor and the disadvantaged. Assisting the refugee and the immigrant. Building social capital for working-class New Yorkers by strengthening public libraries and securing universal access to arts and culture of all kinds.

Layered on these concerns are those my wife, Elizabeth, cares most about, commitments we share. Improving the condition of the city's parks and public spaces more generally. Attending to the welfare of community-based visual arts institutions. Arresting the decline of the quantity and quality of local journalism.

Among the many organizations we support that address these issues are El Museo del Barrio, the Bronx Museum of the Arts, City Limits, Friends of Van Cortlandt Park, New Yorkers for Parks, and a wide variety of community-based advocacy groups.

Through these many vocational and pro bono involvements, connections and obligations, I became accustomed to having my mettle tested. It is invigorating. It is gratifying. It is fulfilling. So far, at least, my personal sell-by date keeps being extended.

When I left Lincoln Center as its president in early 2014, after extending my contract twice at the request of its board of directors, I felt a palpable sense of relief. It had been thirteen years of an eighteen-hour, six-and-a-half-day weekly regimen. Now, there would be no more committee meetings or staff conclaves. Union negotiations, budgets to balance, and contracts to negotiate were in my past. I could bid goodbye to construction managers and employees to support, not to mention the incessant fundraising to propel. The responsibility for the safety of the some seven million people who patronized or visited Lincoln Center each year and for the welfare of thousands of employees and artists we directly employed weighed heavily on me. It was a burden I no longer shouldered.

Friends and colleagues were concerned about my postretirement state of mind. Wouldn't I miss being in the middle of the action? How would I manage the stark transition from a very demanding, structured existence, with almost every waking hour accounted for, to a new professional and personal life written on a tabula rasa? Could I handle no longer being a public figure leading a highly visible organization to becoming just another New Yorker? Did I fret about whether the phone would ever ring again, whether the options I could exercise with my found time would diminish in number and attractiveness?

In essence, my closest friends pressed me to formulate an answer to the very question that opened this book. *Now that you are really grown-up, what is it that you wish to do with your life? Who do you want to become?*

Sound familiar?

Versions of this question turn out to be pertinent not just for children, adolescents, and adults in their prime. They remain just as germane after the AARP (the American Association of Retired

People) solicits you for membership and after your Social Security and Medicare cards arrive in the mail.

That question lingers. It hovers. It clings to you.

Well, I packed my bags, certain of three realities.

Completely comfortable with solitude, I would not miss the glare of publicity associated with running a prominent institution. Nor would I long for the mutterings of New York's ever-present chattering class.

Certain that I had given Lincoln Center my all, I departed without regret. I left behind no would-haves, could-haves, should-haves, or might-haves on my mind or on my conscience. Not a one.

Confident in my accumulated experiences, relationships, and skills, I was not at all concerned about whether I could fill the vacuum granted to me by the gift of time.

And just in case you were wondering, I am not done yet. Life is unfinished.

What I did wonder about was whether I could overcome my lifelong inability to turn down an offer or a request, to utter the three words *no thank you.*

I arranged for plenty to keep me very busy. I was already hard at work on that professional memoir, *They Told Me Not to Take That Job*. Published a little more than a year after my departure from Lincoln Center, this *New York Times* best-seller occasioned a very enjoyable but time-consuming follow-on public speaking schedule. Concurrently, I was retained as a senior adviser to the private equity firm General Atlantic and as a consultant to two of the grantees of the Poses Foundation, the Foundation for Children with Learning Disabilities and the Jed Foundation.

And as if those involvements were not enough, I opted to teach a graduate school course of my own design at Columbia University's School of International Affairs. Soon thereafter, I even accepted an invitation to become the president of the Robin Hood Foundation.

While I professed desiring a lighter workload, this crowded calendar of activity demonstrated otherwise. My occupational cup runneth over. I had taken on too much, too soon.

In a spasm of honest reflection, I even admitted this to myself.

Now, I have settled down. My life is contained in an accordion-like portfolio. There is one compartment reserved for my consulting practice and another for my work as a writer. There is a section set aside for civic and charitable commitments. And one holds papers devoted to helping those individuals and institutions that repair to me for advice and coaching.

This investment of mine in the unrealized potential of gifted people assumes a high priority. Matching the discontented and those who have lost their way to meaningful work, to a charitable mission or a civic cause, is one approach to fixing a world in need of repair. With every placement, I silently celebrate. With every reoriented and redirected professional, the public good is advanced.

Assisting institutions with their strategic, operational, and leadership challenges also takes precedence over other activity. Unlocking organizational energy and unleashing institutional capacity to pursue the general welfare remains a treasured activity.

In continuing to be out in the world, I am very conscious of engaging in what might be called age-appropriate behavior. One of the most important and underestimated qualities in a leader is self-awareness. As you grow older, consider afresh how to conduct yourself when trying to help others. Listen more. Talk less. Coach by asking questions, not issuing directives. Feel free to tell relevant stories drawn from your past experience, but edit them judiciously. Be generous with your time, but do not impose on others. Beware of testing their patience.

Avoid being seen as a know-it-all, or an adviser who is too often looking in the rearview mirror. Do not confine your recommendations to the immediate future, the short term. Defy your contemporaries who only half-kiddingly claim that they no longer buy green bananas, so focused are they on the short term. Remember that "A society grows great when old men plant trees whose shade they know they will never sit in."

It is not just knowledge, experience, and accumulated relationships that can extend your relevance. Critical as well is your personal comportment, how you carry yourself. Vital is whether you keep the future foremost in mind. That is what those who seek your advice care most about.

Coach gently. Guide courteously. Speak frankly. Look forward.

The *how* of your influence is as important as the *what*. In fact, carelessness with the one can actively undermine the other.

And then there's the final part of the portfolio. The one set aside for time with my family and friends. For reading and reflection. For travel. For indulging in the visual and performing arts. For exercise.

I am hoping that this portion will swell as the reality of a lifetime now numbered in years, not decades, reveals itself. It is manifest in the memorial services I attend, the obituaries I read, and the friends and colleagues who are no more.

So now you have it. This is the septuagenarian path I have chosen.

It feels good. It is right for me.

Others opt to stay in place at their current full-time post beyond a traditional retirement date, as measured either by age or by length of tenure. If you are performing well at meaningful work and enjoying it, consider yourself blessed. In such a circumstance, why not stay the course.

To select only examples from the Third Sector, New York City is the better for the longevity of Ellen Futter at the Museum of Natural History, Adam Weinberg at the Whitney Museum, and Glenn Lowry at the Museum of Modern Art. Their institutions have grown in quality, in stature, in physical capacity and attractiveness, and in receptivity to an enlarged and discerning public. Each of these leaders has been employed at the same place for many years. They deserve much of the credit for such accomplishments.

In nonprofit theater, think Todd Haimes, Lynne Meadow and Barry Grove, André Bishop, Carole Rothman, Oskar Eustis, and

Arlene Shuler, respectively, the leaders of the Roundabout, the Manhattan Theatre Club, Lincoln Center Theater, Second Stage Theater, the Public Theater, and City Center. These figures are part of a generation of leaders who have extensively renovated their facilities and/or expanded into additional artistic homes. They have nurtured the proven and the promising, artists of stature and those who are likely to succeed them as our next distinguished class of actors, directors, dramatists, and songwriters. The throbbing excitement of live theater and even the resurgence of Broadway's popularity and artistic worth are due in no small measure to these noteworthy personalities. As we live in a renaissance of theatrical invention, tip your hat to them, among the many others who could have been mentioned.

John Sexton devoted the critical mass of his adult life to New York University, much to its advantage. He left a four-decade tenure as law school dean and president secure in the knowledge that the largest private university in the world was much stronger financially, much higher ranked academically and reputationally, and much more attractive to top-flight students and faculty. Sexton embarked on a global, multicampus strategy that is unique. It knows no equal. Overall, his is an enduring legacy.

Under the leadership of Lee Bollinger, Columbia University is being utterly transformed for the twenty-first century. Its new North Harlem campus is a marvel of ambition and much-needed physical expansion and renewal. Its endowment has more than tripled in size. Its new multidisciplinary initiatives, like mind/brain research and global studies, are expanding even as its traditional departments are strengthening. Few doubt that Lee's tenure—he is already the longest-serving Ivy League president by several years— is a major cause of this proud institution's rejuvenation. Morale is up. Alums are proud. On occasion, even sports teams at Columbia achieve the impossible—they win a game or two.

In social services, to unfairly cite just a single name, consider David Jones. The continuity of his decades-long leadership as president of the Community Service Society has strengthened the delivery of needed programs for poor people, expanded public policy advocacy on their behalf, and achieved demonstrable governmental reform.

These are among my contemporaries who have helped New York City become such a compelling place to work, to study, to visit, and to live.

Still others of comparable age and length of service decide that the torch needs to be passed to a new generation. They depart for different full-time or part-time challenges. Often having set aside sufficient funds for themselves, attention can be focused on charitable and civic preoccupations predominantly.

In this lifelong quest to earn a living in dignified, respectful circumstances and/or helping others less fortunate than you, there will be trials and tribulations. There will be disappointments. Setbacks are not for the young alone.

But in the face of compelling societal needs, you should choose not to neglect contributing to the welfare of others with at least some of your time. How lucky that you are to be able to devote a piece of your autumnal years to easing the plight of those in need. If you select that course of action, whoever you help will never be the same. Nor will you.

Frequently called to mind is a principle apocryphally attributed to Noah. Noah's principle says, "No more credit for predicting rain. Credit only for building arks."

That credit comes in the form of weather that is rarely inclement.

*Start Now*, and the sun is bound to shine on you.

In the precious time remaining, *Start Now*, because that meaningful life is still out there, just waiting for you to grasp it.

# Notes

## Chapter 1

1  Lyrics to the Beatles' "Help!" written by John Lennon and Paul McCartney. "Help!" was released as a single in 1965.

2  Lizzie Widdicombe, "Improving Workplace Culture, One Review at a Time," *New Yorker*, January 20, 2018.

3  David Brooks, "The Moral Bucket List," op-ed column, *New York Times*, April 11, 2015.

4  The latest authoritative data on charitable donations may be found in *Giving USA 2018: The Annual Report on Philanthropy for the Year 2017*. It is researched and written at the Indiana University Lilly Family School of Philanthropy.

5  The data on employment is derived from *Nonprofit Works: An Interactive Database on the US Nonprofit Economy*. It is published by the Johns Hopkins University Center for Civil Society Studies, under the direction of Professor Lester Salamon.

## Chapter 2

1  These typical examples are real-life stories told by guests on the *Axe Files* podcast on CNN and by interviewees on *The David Rubenstein Show: Peer-to-Peer Conversations* that are aired on the Bloomberg network. Repeatedly, now-famous lobbyists, politicians, CEOs, media moguls, and VIPs report on how their careers were shaped early on by fortuitous circumstances that they were in a position to benefit from. The lesson? Be willing to take on any job in a work setting. Be useful, available, cheerful, and hardworking.

2  More than a few how-to books on building and maintaining networks are available for review. When thoughts turn to who can be most helpful to you in a job search, consider relatives, friends of relatives, spousal connections, current colleagues, members of professional and social organizations, current and former customers and clients, parents of your children's friends, neighbors past and present, people you went to school with, people you have worked with in

the past, people in your religious congregation, former teachers and employers, people you socialize with, people who provide services to you, and people with whom you interact on Facebook or LinkedIn. These examples are drawn from pages 78 and 79 of a book coauthored by Keith Ferrazzi with Tahl Raz and entitled *Never Eat Alone: And Other Secrets to Success, One Relationship at a Time* (New York: Crown, 2014).

3   Richard Holbrooke, *To End a War* (New York: Random House, 1998).

4   This first-person account is drawn from seventeen months of personal experience watching Holbrooke in action, close up, and conversing with him every few weeks. It is consistent with an extraordinary recently published biography. George Packer's *Our Man: Richard Holbrooke and the End of the American Century* treats his larger-than-life subject as a metaphor for the decline of US influence abroad. By contrast, what I witnessed was only one dimension of Holbrooke's energetic, ingenious, and crafty diplomatic skill. As an advocate for the victims of HIV/AIDS, for immigrants, and for refugees, and as a statesman who fully understood the power of nongovernment organizations, Holbrooke had no equal.

5   This quote is a slight modification of Justice Oliver Wendell Holmes, who wrote that "In the life of the law, an ounce of experience is worth a pound of logic."

6   See Bill Barnett, *The Strategic Career: Let Business Principles Guide You* (Stanford, California: Stanford University Press, 2015); Liz Ryan, *Reinvention Roadmap: Break the Rules to Get the Job You Want and Career You Deserve* (Dallas, Texas: Ben Bella Books, Inc., 2016); and Bill Burnett and Dale Evans, *Designing Your Life: How to Build a Well-Lived, Joyful Life* (New York: Alfred A. Knopf, 2017).

7   This quotation is attributed to Helmuth von Moltke the Elder, chief of staff of the Prussian Army before World War I.

## Chapter 3

1   See Suzanne Bouffard, *The Most Important Year: Pre-Kindergarten and the Future of Our Children* (New York: Avery, 2017), and Amanda Ripley, *The Smartest Kids in the World and How They Got That Way* (New York: Simon and Schuster, 2013).

2   See Jason DeParle's thorough report "As Washington Limps Along, Head Start Thrives: Unheralded Bipartisan Success in a Bitterly Polarized Moment," *New York Times*, February 5, 2019. Also see Leslie Brody's article in the May 14, 2019 *Wall Street Journal* entitled "Long-Term Study Shows Free Pre-K Helps Low-Income Students, and Their Children." Brody reports on the remarkable findings and conclusions of Nobel laureate James Heckman. His research reveals that the positive impact of preschool programs stretch over a lifetime. In following for over five decades a sample of those who enrolled and matriculated, he argues that early childhood education can do no less than break the cycle of poverty.

3 See "It's Not Just A Diaper Change—The Educators' Spin on It," and "Learning and Development: Infants Birth to 12 Months," Better Brains for Babies website, Georgia Department of Human Services.

4 For some of the best of this growing body of work, see George Anders, *You Can Do Anything: The Surprising Power of a "Useless" Liberal Arts Education* (New York: Little Brown and Company, 2017); Frank Bruni, *Where You Go Is Not Who You'll Be: An Antidote to the College Admissions Mania* (New York: Grand Central Publishing, 2016); Andrew Delbanco, *College: What It Was, Is, and Should Be* (Princeton, New Jersey: Princeton University Press, 2012); Randall Stross, *A Practical Education: Why Liberal Arts Majors Make Great Employees* (Stanford, California: Stanford University Press, 2017); and Fareed Zakaria, *In Defense of a Liberal Education* (New York: W.W. Norton and Company, 2015).

5 See Herb Childress, *The Adjunct Underclass: How America's Colleges Betrayed Their Faculty, Their Students, and Their Mission* (Chicago: University of Chicago Press), 2019.

6 See Fareed Zakaria, *In Defense of a Liberal Education*, 103.

7 See George Anders, *You Can Do Anything: The Surprising Power of a "Useless" Liberal Arts Education*. New York: Little Brown and Company, 2017, 152–154.

8 Randall Stross, *A Practical Education: Why Liberal Arts Majors Make Great Employees*. Stanford, California: Redwood Press, 2017, 225.

9 Op. cit., 238–239.

10 See George Anders, *You Can Do Anything: The Surprising Power of a "Useless" Liberal Arts Education*, 134.

11 See Reynold Levy, *Contending Approaches to Contemporary American Foreign Policy* (New York: The Free Press, 1975).

12 Tom Friedman, *The "Next America,"* opinion, *New York Times*, December 4, 2018.

# Chapter 5

1 How you present yourself physically, emotionally, and intellectually is a subject well covered by Amy Cuddy in *Presence: Bringing Your Boldest Self to Your Biggest Challenges* (New York: Little Brown and Company, 2015).

2 See Daniel B. Baer, "Condoleezza Rice and Bob Gates Should Apologize for Endorsing Rex Tillerson," *Foreign Policy*, August 21, 2017.

# Chapter 6

1 Ray Dalio, *Principles* (New York: Simon and Schuster, 2017), 404.

2 Laszlo Bock, *Work Rules!: Insights from Google That Will Transform How You Live and Lead* (New York: Twelve, 2015).

3    Geoff Colvin, *Talent Is Overrated: What Really Separates World-Class Performers from Everybody Else* (New York: Penguin, 2008), 12–13.

4    Timothy Butler and James Wardroop, "Job Sculpting: The Art of Retaining Your Best People," in *On Finding and Keeping the Best People* (Boston: Harvard Business School Publishing, 1994).

5    Laszlo Bock, *Work Rules!: Insights From Inside Google That Will Transform How You Live and Lead* (New York: Twelve, 2015).

     Google's method of attracting, assessing, and cultivating new hires is highly unusual. It does not allow managers to select their own teams, even their own direct reports. Multiple group interviews convened by employees from many disciplines over many weeks, even months, with the CEO, Larry Page, as the final reviewer for *every* candidate is the norm!

     This glacial hiring process, its consumption of tens of thousands of hours of time, its undermining of supervisory autonomy and judgment, its testing of the frustration tolerance of candidates and internal referrers all has caused Google to reconsider and modify the methods used. But in reading Bock closely, one searches in vain for really significant remedial measures. To hire and be hired at Google remains an unnecessarily confusing, exhausting, and, in many respects, countercultural and counterproductive exercise.

6    Bock argues for focusing less on the firm to be retained than on the experience, character, and judgment of the lead recruiter proposed for the search.

     …there's more variance in quality within search firms than across search firms, so selecting the individual consultants you work with is more critical than selecting the company.

     See Laszlo Bock, *Work Rules!*, 84.

7    Kevin Ryan, "Building a Team of A Players," in *How I Did It: Lessons from the Front Lines of Business*, ed. Daniel McGinn (Boston: Harvard Business Review Press, 2014).

8    For background on the appointment of Gregory J. Vincent and his subsequent resignation nine months later due to allegations of plagiarism in his doctoral dissertation, please see the article by Fernanda Zamudio-Suarez in the April 13, 2018, issue of *The Chronicle of Higher Education*.

9    For background on the embarrassing resignation of Leslie Cohen Berlowitz, who reportedly resigned from her post as the president of the American Academy of Arts and Sciences because she had falsely claimed to have been awarded a doctoral degree, please see Jennifer Schuessler writing in the *New York Times* of July 25, 2013, under the headline "Embattled President of the American Academy of Arts and Sciences to Resign."

10   An excellent example is Ellen Futter, who moved from a successful tenure as the president of Barnard College to become the CEO of the Museum of Natural History, where she has been a transformational leader.

11   Gregory Long, the recently retired president of the New York Botanical Garden after a quarter century of outstanding service, had moved to that post from being a superb director of development for the New York Public Library, reporting to its legendary president, Vartan Gregorian.

## Chapter 7

1 As quoted in Philip Delves Broughton, *Life's a Pitch: What the World's Best Sales People Can Teach Us All* (New York: Penguin, 2012), 255.

2 This formulation comes from Bill Burnett and Dave Evans, *Designing Your Life: How to Build a Well-Lived, Joyful Life* (New York: Alfred A. Knopf, 2017), 92.

3 There are recent books written to be helpful to women as the target audience on matters like promotion and compensation. They are practical, down-to-earth, and encouraging. I recommend Mika Brzezinski's *Know Your Value: Women, Money, and Getting What You're Worth* (New York: Hachette, 2018); Mika Brzezinski and Daniela Pierre-Bravo, *Earn It! Know Your Value and Grow Your Career, in Your 20s and Beyond* (New York: Hachette, 2019); and Katty Kay and Claire Shipman, *The Confidence Code: The Science and Art of Self-Assurance—What Women Should Know* (New York: Harper Business, 2018).

4 A solid source of guidance to the new institutional leader can be found in James Citrin's and Thomas Neff's *You're in Charge—Now What?* (New York: Random House, 2005).

5 This description of how I approached my first year as the CEO of Lincoln Center is elaborated on in my book *They Told Me Not to Take That Job: Tumult, Betrayal, Heroics, and the Transformation of Lincoln Center*. New York: Public Affairs, 2015, 265–304.

6 Ibid.

7 William Faulkner, *Requiem for a Nun* (New York: Random House, 1951).

8 See Adam Nagourney, "'What Will I Not Miss?' In California, a Long Farewell from Jerry Brown," *New York Times*, January 3, 2019, A14.

9 This is the dominant theme of Cal Newport's *So Good They Can't Ignore You: Why Skills Trump Passion in the Quest for Work You Love* (New York: Hachette, 2012).

10 Malcolm Gladwell, *Outliers* (New York: Little, Brown and Company, 2011).

11 Stephen Joel Trachtenberg, Gerald B. Kauvar, and E. Grady Bogue, *Presidencies Derailed: Why University Leaders Fail and How to Prevent It* (Baltimore: Johns Hopkins University Press, 2013).

## Chapter 8

1 Samuel Johnson, *The History of Rasselas: Prince of Abissinia*, ed. Thomas Keymer, (Oxford: Oxford University Press, reprint edition, 2009), 19.

2 Patricia O'Toole, *In the Words of Theodore Roosevelt: Quotations from the Man in the Arena* (Ithaca, New York: Cornell University Press, 2012), 186.

3 Read cover-to-cover Reid Hoffman and Ben Casnocha, *The Start-Up of You: Adapt to the Future, Invest in Yourself, and Transform Your Career* (New York: Crown Business, 2012).

4    Richard Langworth, *Churchill by Himself: The Definitive Collection of Quotations* (Public Affairs; first edition, 2008), 578.

5    See David Leonhardt's op-ed column (*New York Times*, January 28, 2019, A23).

6    For two influential and up-to-date sources that identify firms providing benefits unusual in their quality, quantity, and impact, read *Fortune*'s annual March issue "100 Best Companies to Work For/2018" and *Forbes*'s annual report on "Just Capital." The latter initiative was conceived and largely underwritten by hedge fund titan Paul Tudor Jones. It is designed to comprehensively compare and contrast company performance on many social indicators, including, importantly, and not least, how employees are treated.

7    See the CEO Jamie Dimon's annual newsletter, 2019, and, more generally, note this trend: "Starting in the mid-1970s, banks rapidly increased their use of ATMs… One might expect such automation to decimate the ranks of bank tellers, but in fact the number of bank teller jobs did not decrease as the ATMs were rolled out." Quite the contrary, as Dimon's leading indicator expression of intent to expand branches and the number of tellers, reveals. James Bessen, "Tellers, Toil and Technology," *ATM Marketplace*, March 12, 2015.

8    See Deborah Block, "U.S. Independent Book Stores Thriving and Growing," *VOA News*, April 10, 2019, and the report of the industry trade group the American Book Sellers Association has quoted in Susan Kitchen's report in the *Wall Street Journal* of April 29, 2019, entitled "How One Independent Book Store Has Survived—Even Thrived—in the Age of Amazon, the Next Chapter."

9    For Broadway, in the 2017–2018 season, 13.8 million tickets were sold, the second-highest total ever. In that same year, 1,125 Broadway shows toured America, also the second-highest total. Such figures are supplied by the Broadway League. As for movies, 1.3 billion tickets were sold in the last recorded season of 2018, roughly the same as in 2005, even in the face of the explosive growth of at-home streaming options. See Nash Information Services, "The Numbers: Where Data and the Movie Business Meet, 2019."

10   Audiobooks are the fastest-growing segment of the digital publishing industry with $2.5 billion in sales in 2017. More than a quarter of the US population has listened to an audiobook in the last 12 months. According to the American Publishers Association, from 2016 to 2017 there was a 29 percent increase in the number of audiobooks produced, to 79,000. Meanwhile, e-book sales, the much-touted technological innovation, had declined by 5 percent in the same period.

# Chapter 9

1    See Victor E. Frankel, *Man's Search for Meaning* (Boston: Beacon Press, 2006).

2   E. B. White, "E. B. White: Notes and Comment by Author, interview with
    Israel Shenker, July 11, 1969; *New York Times*," in *In the Words of E. B. White:
    Quotations From America's Most Companionable of Writers*, ed. Martha White
    (Ithaca, New York: Cornell University Press, 2011), 148.
3   Wisława Szymborska was a well-known Polish poet who lived from 1923 to
    2012.
4   See Susan Adams, "Most Americans Are Unhappy at Work," *Forbes*, June 20,
    2014. Ms. Adams draws from Conference Board studies in job satisfaction that
    are issued annually.
5   Julius Rosenwald, speech delivered in 1923.
6   See Adam Smith, *The Theory of Moral Sentiments* (New York: Kelpaz Publica-
    tions, 2017).
7   See Arthur C. Brooks, *Who Really Cares* (New York: Basic Books, 2006),
    Chapter 7, "Charity Makes You Healthy, Happy, and Rich," 137–160.
8   Ibid.
9   Pierre Omidyar, "Innovating the Business Model of Social Change," in *How
    I Did It: Lessons from the Front Line of Business*, ed. Daniel McGinn (Boston:
    Harvard Business School Publishing, 2014).

# Chapter 10

1   Winston Lord, *Kissinger on Kissinger: Reflections on Diplomacy, Grand Strategy,
    and Leadership* (New York: All Points Books, 2019).
2   Here are just fifteen examples of my former very close colleagues at the 92nd
    Street Y, AT&T, the International Rescue Committee, and Lincoln Center
    who moved on to other significant professional roles and responsibilities. Becca
    Arnold: senior director, strategy, Ross Stores; Kara Medoff Barnett: executive
    director, American Ballet Theatre; Mark Bartolini: director, Office of Foreign
    Affairs Disaster Assistance at the US Agency for International Development;
    Clive Chang: director, strategy and business development, Disney Theatri-
    cal Group; Tom Dunn: executive director, Southampton Arts Center; Kristy
    Geslain: senior producer, ALL ARTS, WNET; Russell Granet: president,
    New 42nd Street; Lauren Kiel: executive director, Center for Ballet and the
    Arts at New York University; Lee Koffler: former associate of McKinsey and
    now chief operating officer of the Voleon Group; Sharon Gersten Luckman:
    former executive director, Twyla Tharp Dance Foundation and Alvin Ailey
    Dance Company; Tim McClimon: executive director, Second Stage Theatre,
    and president, American Express Foundation; Shilla Kim Parker: former
    chief of staff to Ben Sherwood, former president of Disney|ABC Television
    Group, and founder of new start-up, Thrilling; John Ruskay: former president,
    Federation of Jewish Philanthropies of New York; Jennifer Houston Scripps:
    director, Office of Cultural Affairs, City of Dallas; Roanna Shorofsky: founder

and former CEO, Abraham Heschel School; and Henry Wainhouse: attorney, Jones Day.

3 The quote is attributed to President Theodore Roosevelt.

4 Excerpt from a speech delivered by Robert Kennedy in South Africa, 1966.

## Chapter 11

1 Lucy Larcom, "Plant a Tree," in *Great Poems by American Women: An Anthology*, ed. Susan L. Rattiner (Mineola, New York: Dover Publications, Inc., 2012), 73–74.

# Selected Bibliography

Anders, George. *You Can Do Anything: The Surprising Power of a "Useless" Liberal Arts Education*. Boston: Little, Brown and Company, 2017.

Barnett, Bill. *The Strategic Career: Let Business Principles Guide You*. Stanford, California: Stanford University Press, 2015.

Baumol, Williams J., Joan Jeffri, and David Throsby. *Making Change: Facilitating the Transitions of Dancers to Post-Performance Careers*. New York: The Advance Project, 2004.

Bock, Laszlo. *Work Rules!* New York: Twelve, 2010.

Bolles, Richard N. *What Color Is Your Parachute? A Practical Manual for Job-Hunters and Career-Changers*. Berkeley: Ten Speed Press, 2017.

Bouffard, Suzanne. *The Most Important Year: Pre-Kindergarten and the Future of Our Children*. New York: Avery, 2017.

Bowen, William G. *The Board Book: An Insider's Guide for Directors and Trustees*. New York: W.W. Norton and Company, 2008.

Brooks, Arthur C. *Who Really Cares*. New York: Basic Books, 2006.

Broughton, Philip Delves. *The Art of the Sale: Learning from the Masters about the Business of Life*. New York: Penguin, 2012.

Bruni, Frank. *Where You Go Is Not Who You'll Be: An Antidote to the College Admissions Mania*. New York: Grand Central Publishing, 2015.

Brzezinski, Mika. *Know Your Value: Women, Money, and Getting What You're Worth*. New York: Hachette, 2018.

Brzezinski, Mika, with Daniela Pierre-Bravo. *Earn It!: Know Your Value and Grow Your Career, In Your 20s and Beyond*. New York: Hachette, 2019.

Burnett, Bill, and Dave Evans. *Designing Your Life: How to Build a Well-Lived, Joyful Life*. New York: Alfred A. Knopf, 2016.

Carey, Dennis, Dominic Barton, and Ram Charan. *Talent Wins: The New Playbook for Putting People First*. Boston: Harvard Business Review, 2018.

Cavoulacos, Alexandra, and Kathryn Minshew. *The New Rules of Work: The Modern Playbook for Navigating Your Career*. New York: Crown Business, 2017.

Charan, Ram. *Boards That Deliver: Advancing Corporate Governance from Compliance to Competitive Advantage*. New York: John Wiley and Sons, 2005.

Charan, Ram. *Owning Up: The 14 Questions Every Board Member Needs to Ask*. San Francisco: John Wiley and Sons, 2009.

Childress, Herb. *The Adjunct Underclass: How America's Colleges Betrayed Their Faculty, Their Students, and Their Mission*. Chicago: University of Chicago Press, 2019.

Citrin, James M. *The Career Playbook: Essential Advice for Today's Aspiring Young Professional*. New York: Crown Business, 2015.

Citrin, James M. *The Dynamic Path*. New York: Rodale, 2007.

Citrin, James M., and Julie Hembruck Daum. *You Need a Leader—Now What? How to Choose the Best Person for Your Organization*. New York: Crown Business, 2011.

Colvin, Geoff. *Talent Is Overrated: What Really Separates World-Class Performers from Everybody Else*. New York: Portfolio, 2010.

Cuddy, Amy. *Presence: Bringing Your Boldest Self to Your Biggest Challenges*. New York: Little, Brown and Co., 2015.

Dalio, Ray. *Principles*. New York: Simon and Schuster, 2017.

Delbanco, Andrew. *College: What It Was, Is, and Should Be*. Princeton, New Jersey: Princeton University Press, 2012.

Dietz, Nathan E., Saunji Fyffe, and Brice S. McKeever. *The Nonprofit Almanac: The Essential Facts and Figures for Managers, Researchers, and Volunteers*. Washington, D.C.: Urban Institute Press, 2017 (ninth edition).

Drucker, Peter F. *Managing the Nonprofit Organization: Principles and Practices*. New York: Harper and Collins, 1990.

Ferrazzi, Keith, with Tahl Raz. *Never Eat Alone: And Other Secrets to Success, One Relationship at a Time*. New York: Crown Business, 2014.

Gardner, John. *Self-Renewal: The Individual and the Innovative Society*. New York: W.W. Norton and Company, 1995.

Galloway, Scott. *The Four: The Hidden DNA of Amazon, Apple, Facebook, and Google*. New York: Random House, 2017.

Gilbert, Daniel. *Stumbling on Happiness*. New York: Random House, 2006.

Gladwell, Malcolm. *Outliers*. New York: Little, Brown and Company, 2011.

Golden, Seth. *Purple Cow: Transform Your Business by Being Remarkable*. New York: Portfolio, 2013.

Harvard Business Review. *On Finding and Keeping the Best People*. Boston: Harvard Business School Publishing, 2001.

Hoffman, Reid, and Ben Casnocha. *The Start-Up of You: Adapt to the Future, Invest in Yourself, and Transform Your Career*. New York: Crown Business, 2012.

Holiday, Ryan. *The Obstacle Is the Way: The Timeless Art of Turning Trials into Triumph*. New York: Penguin, 2014.

Ingram, Richard T., and associates. *Governing Independent Colleges and Universities: A Handbook for Trustees, Chief Executives, and Other Campus Leaders*. San Francisco: Jossey-Bass Publishers, 1993.

Kay, Katty, and Claire Shipman. *The Confidence Code: The Science and Art of Self-Assurance—What Women Should Know*. New York: Harper Business, 2018.

Levy, Reynold. *They Told Me Not to Take That Job: Tumult, Betrayal, Heroics, and the Transformation of Lincoln Center*. New York: Public Affairs, 2015.

Levy, Reynold. *Yours for the Asking: An Indispensable Guide to Fundraising and Management.* New York: John Wiley & Sons, Inc., 2008.

Lewis, Mike. *When to Jump: If the Job You Have Isn't the Life You Want.* New York: Henry Holt and Company, 2018.

Lore, Nicholas. *The Pathfinder: How to Choose or Change Your Career for a Lifetime of Satisfaction and Success.* New York: Simon and Schuster, 2011.

Maister, David H., Charles H. Green, and Robert M. Galford. *The Trusted Advisor.* New York: Free Press, 2000.

McAdam, Terry W. *Careers in the Nonprofit Sector: Doing Well by Doing Good.* Washington D.C.: The Taft Group, 1986.

McGinn, Daniel, ed. *How I Did It: Lessons from the Front Lines of Business.* Boston: Harvard Business Review Press, 2014.

McRaven, William H. *Make Your Bed: Little Things That Can Change Your Life and Maybe the World.* New York: Hachette, 2017.

Minshew, Kathryn, and Alexandra Cavoulacos. *The New Rules of Work: The Modern Playbook for Navigating Your Career.* New York: Crown Business, 2017.

Neff, Thomas J., and James M. Citrin. *You're in Charge—Now What? The 8-Point Plan.* New York: Three Rivers Press, 2005.

Newport, Cal. *So Good They Can't Ignore You: Why Skills Trump Passion in the Quest for Work You Love.* Boston: Little, Brown and Company, 2016.

Ogilvy, David. *The Unpublished David Ogilvy.* London: The Ogilvy Group, 1986.

O'Toole, James. *Creating the Good Life: Applying Aristotle's Wisdom to Find Meaning and Happiness.* New York: Rodale, 2005.

Packer, George. *Our Man: Richard Holbrooke and the End of the American Century.* New York: Alfred A. Knopf, 2019.

Riesman, David, and Judith Block McLaughlin. *Choosing a College President: Opportunities and Constraints.* Princeton: The Carnegie Foundation for the Advancement of Teaching, 1990.

Ripley, Amanda. *The Smartest Kids in the World and How They Got That Way.* New York: Simon and Schuster, 2013.

Rubin, Gretchen. *The Happiness Project.* New York: Harper Collins, 2015.

Rubin, Gretchen. *Better Than Before.* New York: Broadway Books, 2013.

Ryan, Liz. *Reinvention Roadmap.* Dallas, Texas: Ben Bella Books, Inc., 2016.

Sandberg, Sheryl. *Lean In: Women, Work, and the Will to Lead.* New York: Alfred A. Knopf, 2013.

Schlesinger, Leonard A., and Charles F. Keifer. *Just Start.* Boston: Harvard Business Review Press, 2012.

Sims, Peter. *Little Bets: How Breakthrough Ideas Emerge from Small Discoveries.* New York: Free Press, 2011.

Stross, Randall. *A Practical Education: Why Liberal Arts Majors Make Great Employees.* San Francisco: Redwood Press, 2017.

Trachtenberg, Stephen J., Gerald B. Kaurer, and E. Grady Bogue. *Presidencies Derailed: Why University Leaders Fail and How to Prevent It*. Baltimore: The Johns Hopkins University Press, 2013.

Yate, Martin. *Knock 'Em Dead: Hiring the Best—Proven Tactics for Successful Employee Selection*. Avon, Massachusetts: Adams Media, 2014 (sixth edition).

Young, Dennis, and Lilly Cohen. *Careers for Dreamers and Doers: A Guide to Management Careers in the Nonprofit Sector*. New York: The Foundation Center, 1989.

Zakaria, Fareed. *In Defense of a Liberal Education*. New York: W.W. Norton and Company, 2015.

Zander, Alvin. *Making Boards Effective: The Dynamics of Nonprofit Governing Boards*. San Francisco: Jossey-Bass Publishers, 1993.

# About the Author

A frequent recipient of awards and honorary degrees, Reynold Levy maintains a busy schedule of public speaking and consulting to commercial, nonprofit, and philanthropic clients. His last book, *They Told Me Not to Take That Job: Tumult, Betrayal, Heroics, and the Transformation of Lincoln Center*, was a *New York Times* bestseller.

In a career devoted to public service, Reynold was most recently the president of the Robin Hood Foundation. Previously he served as the president of Lincoln Center for the Performing Arts from March 1, 2002, to January 31, 2014. Reynold also served as the president of the International Rescue Committee, a senior officer at AT&T and the president of the AT&T Foundation, the executive director of the 92nd Street Y, and the staff director of the task force on the New York City fiscal crisis. He has taught at New York University, Columbia University, and Harvard Business School.

Levy is a member of the Council on Foreign Relations, a trustee of the Charles H. Revson Foundation and the American Ballet Theatre, and a Fellow of the American Academy of Arts and Sciences. He also is the lead director of First Republic Bank.

A graduate of Hobart College, Phi Beta Kappa, Levy earned a PhD in government and foreign affairs from the University of Virginia and a law degree from Columbia University.

*Start Now: Because That Meaningful Job Is Out There, Just Waiting For You* is his fifth book.

# Index

Page numbers followed by *n* refer to notes.